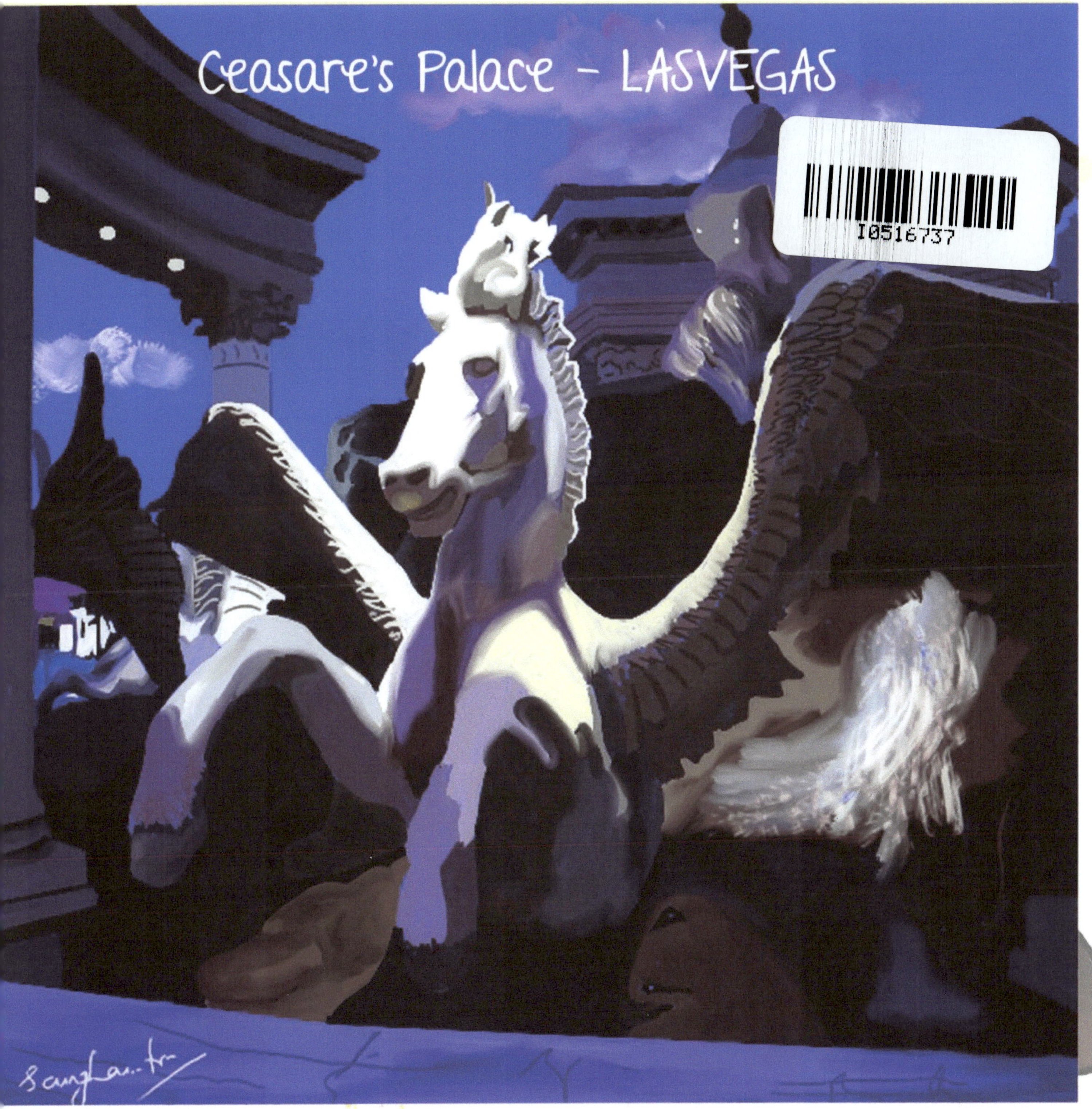
Ceasare's Palace - LASVEGAS

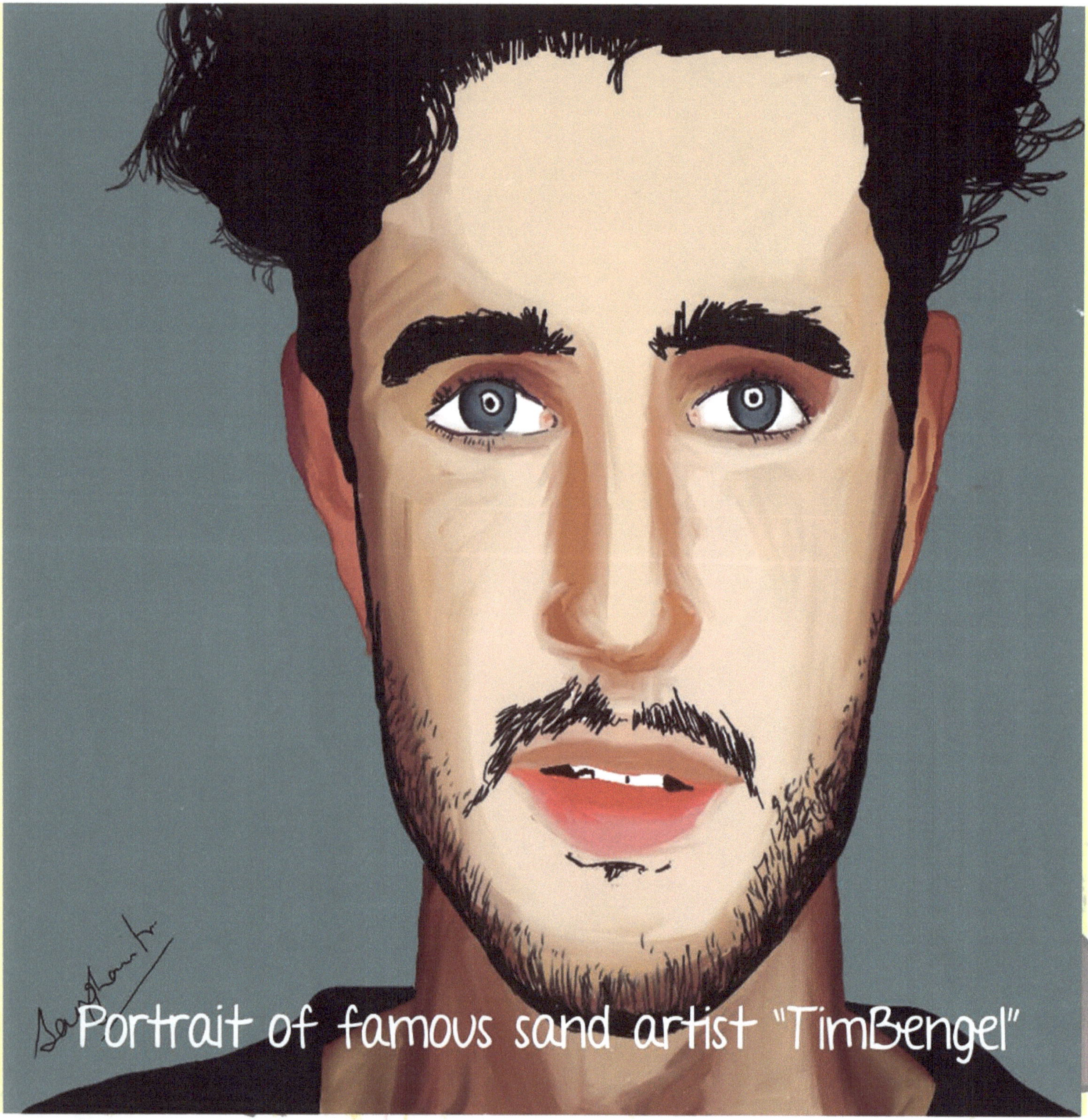
Portrait of famous sand artist "TimBengel"

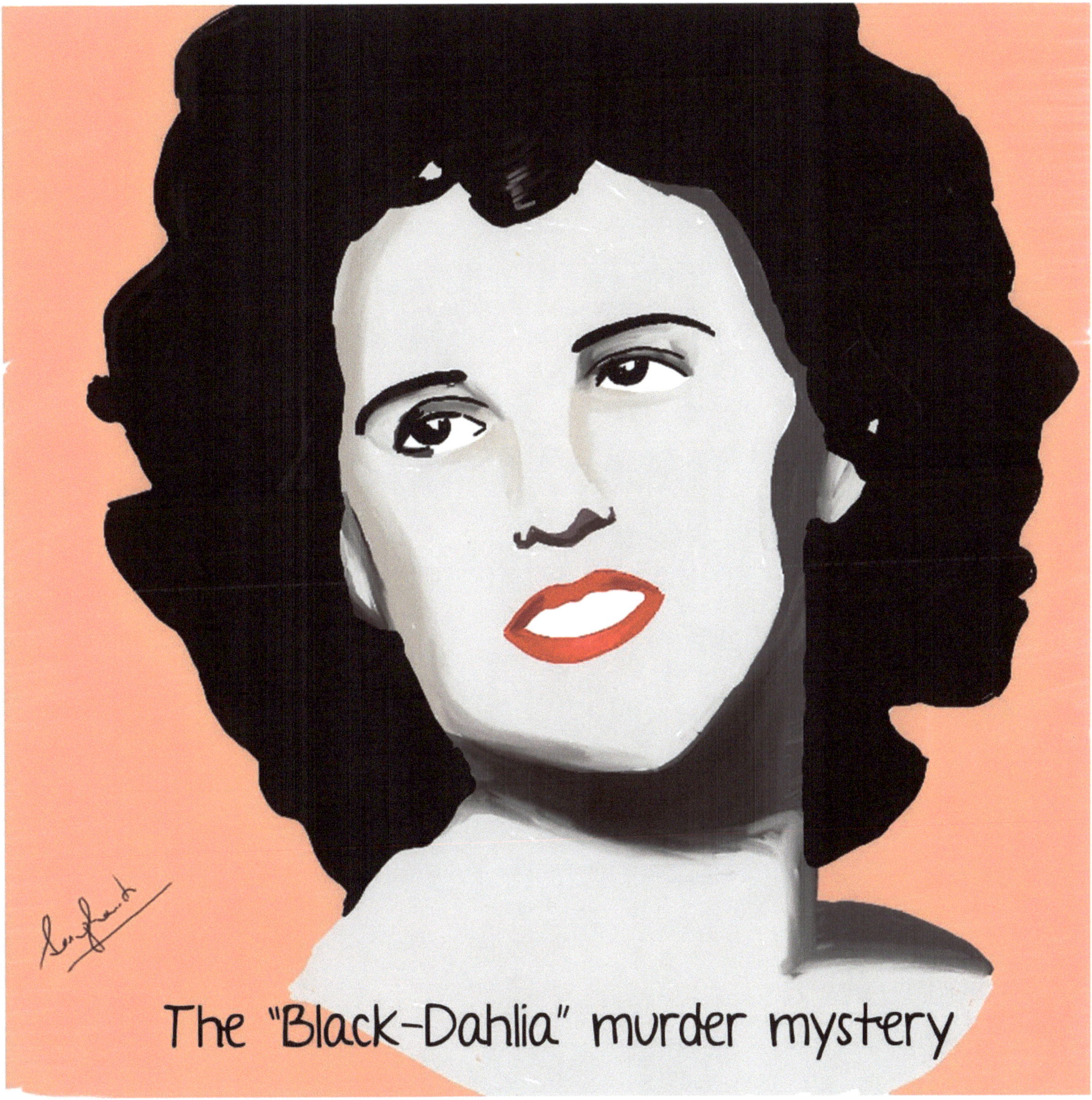
The "Black-Dahlia" murder mystery

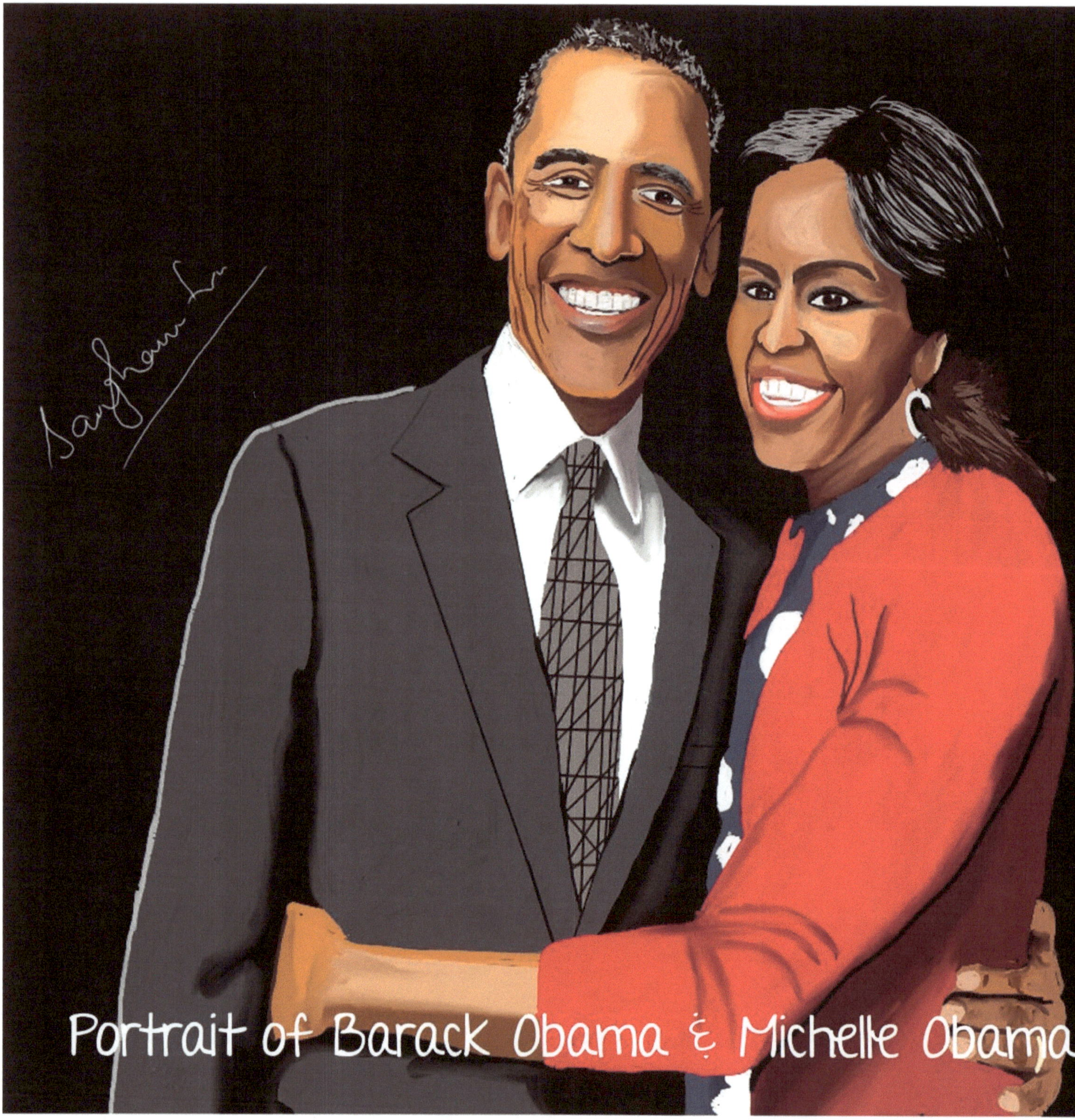

Portrait of Barack Obama & Michelle Obama

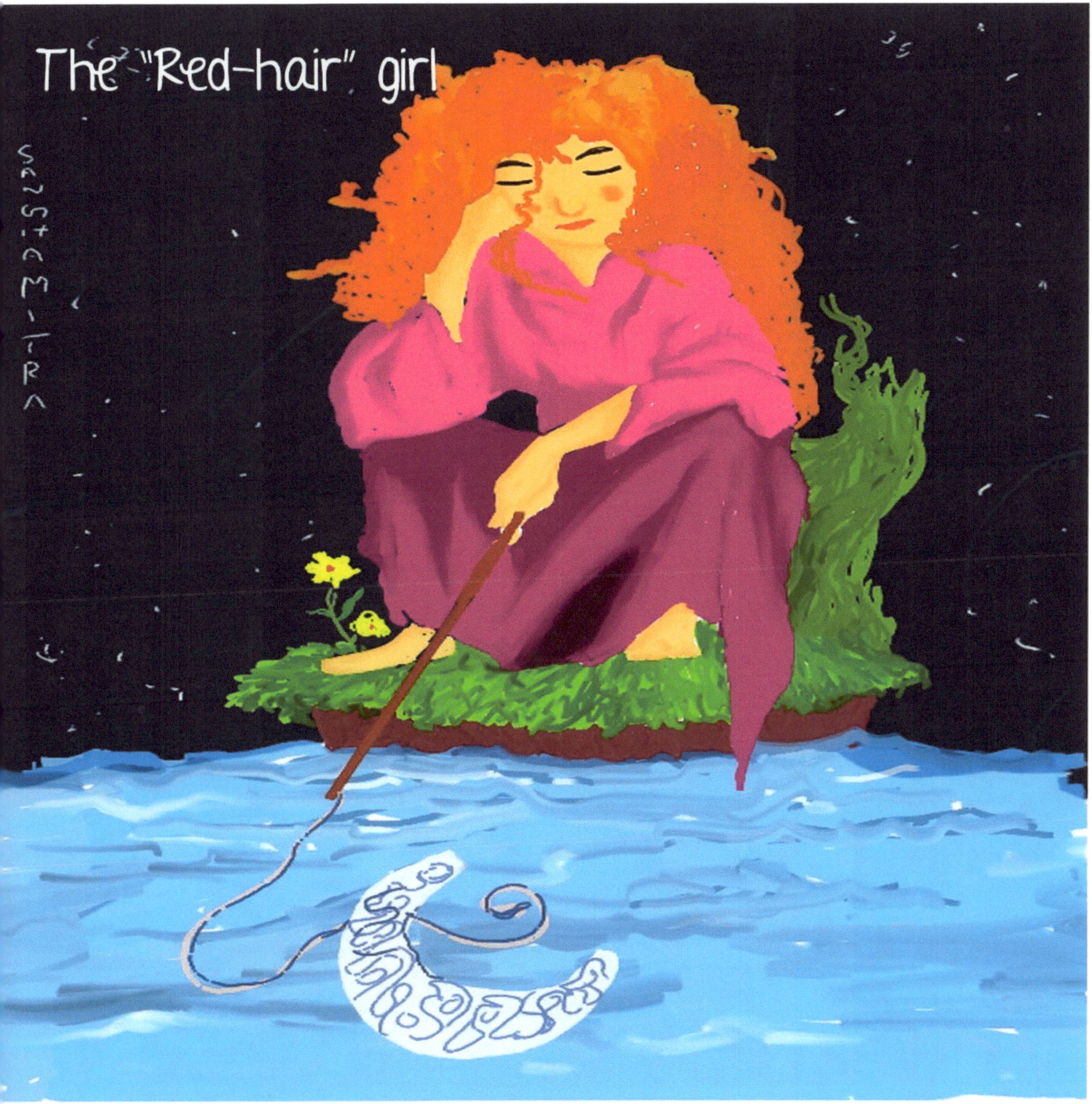
The "Red-hair" girl

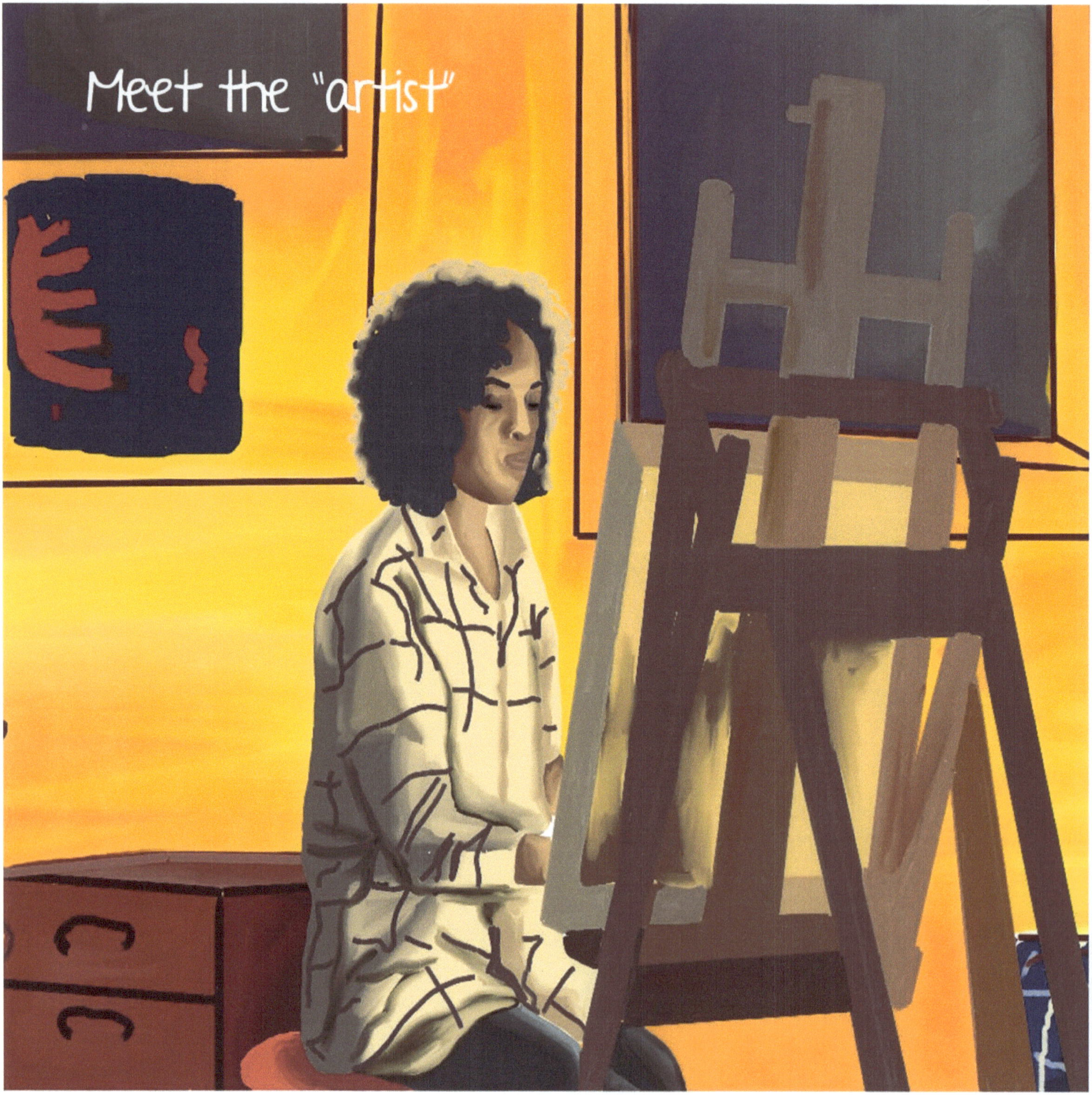
Meet the "artist"

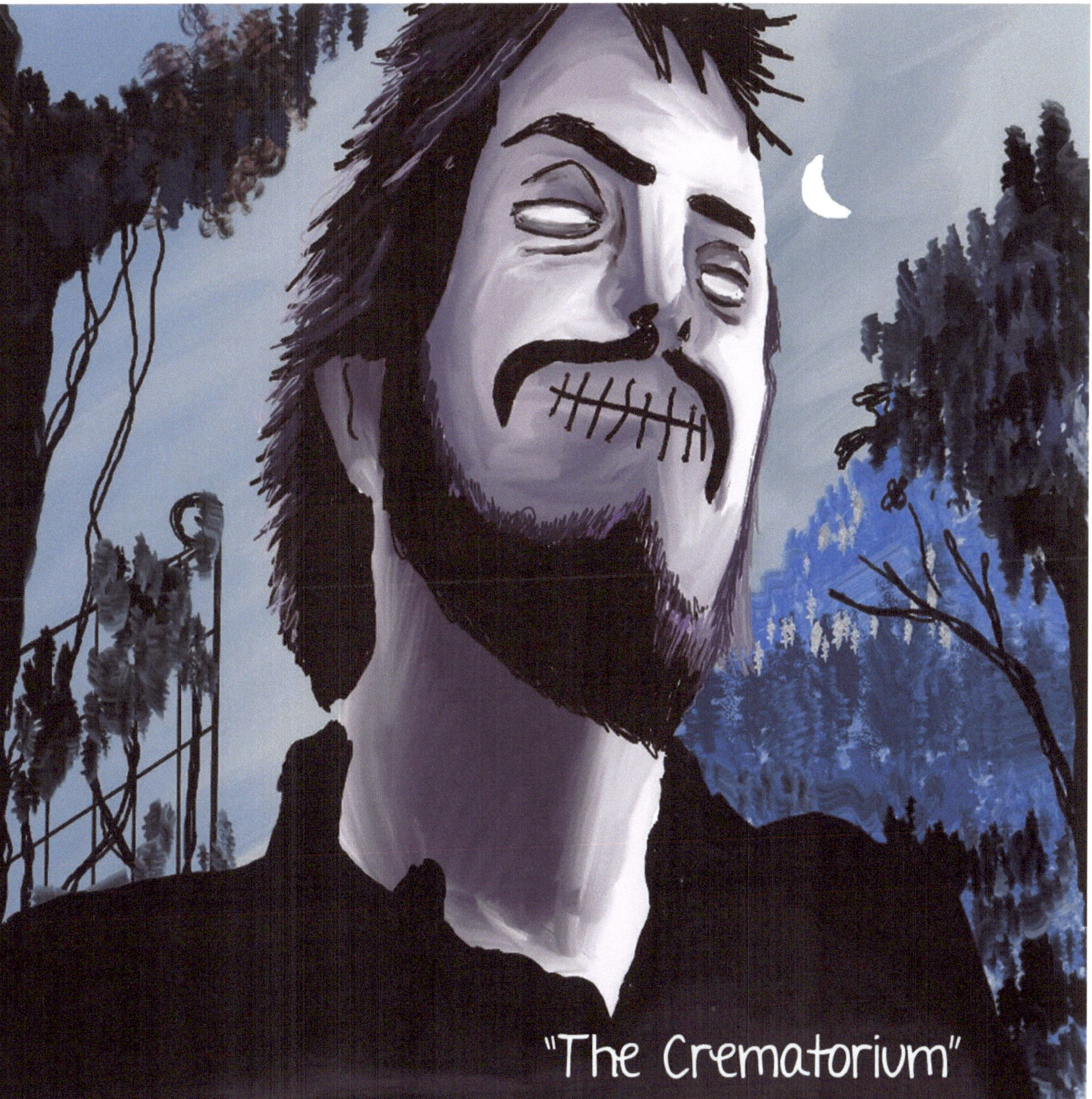
"The Crematorium"

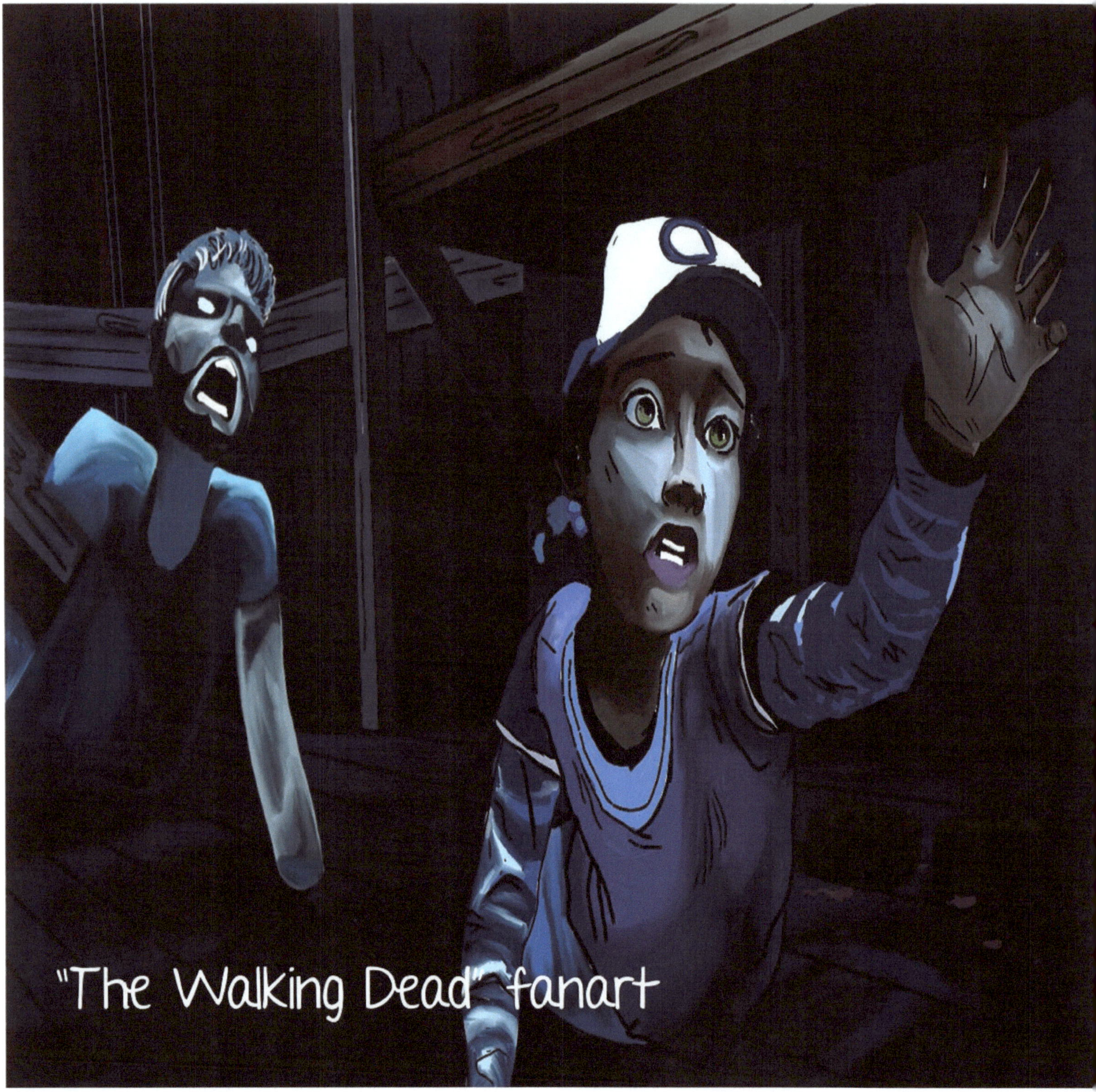
"The Walking Dead" fanart

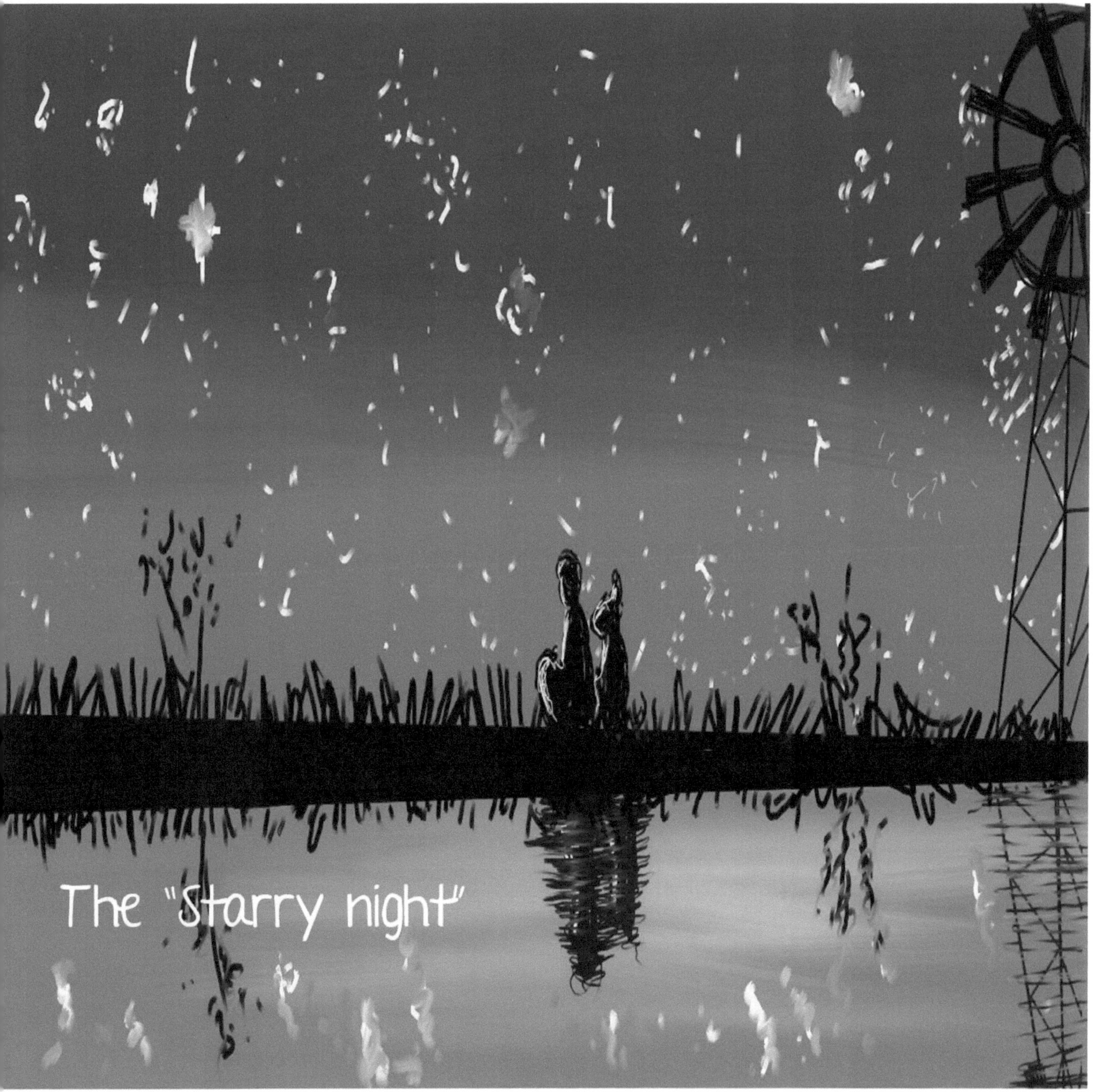
The "Starry night"

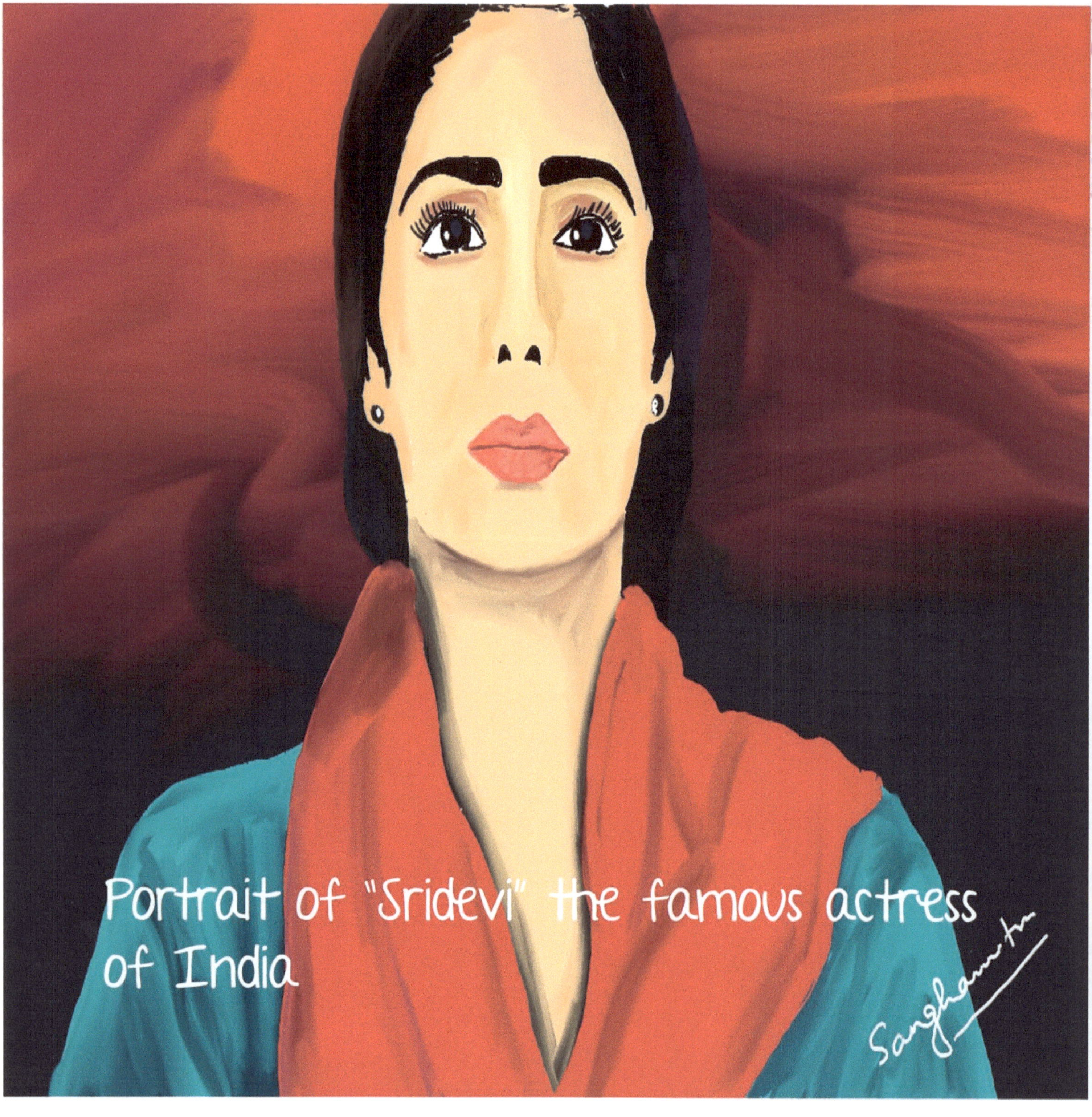
Portrait of "Sridevi" the famous actress of India
Sanghamitra

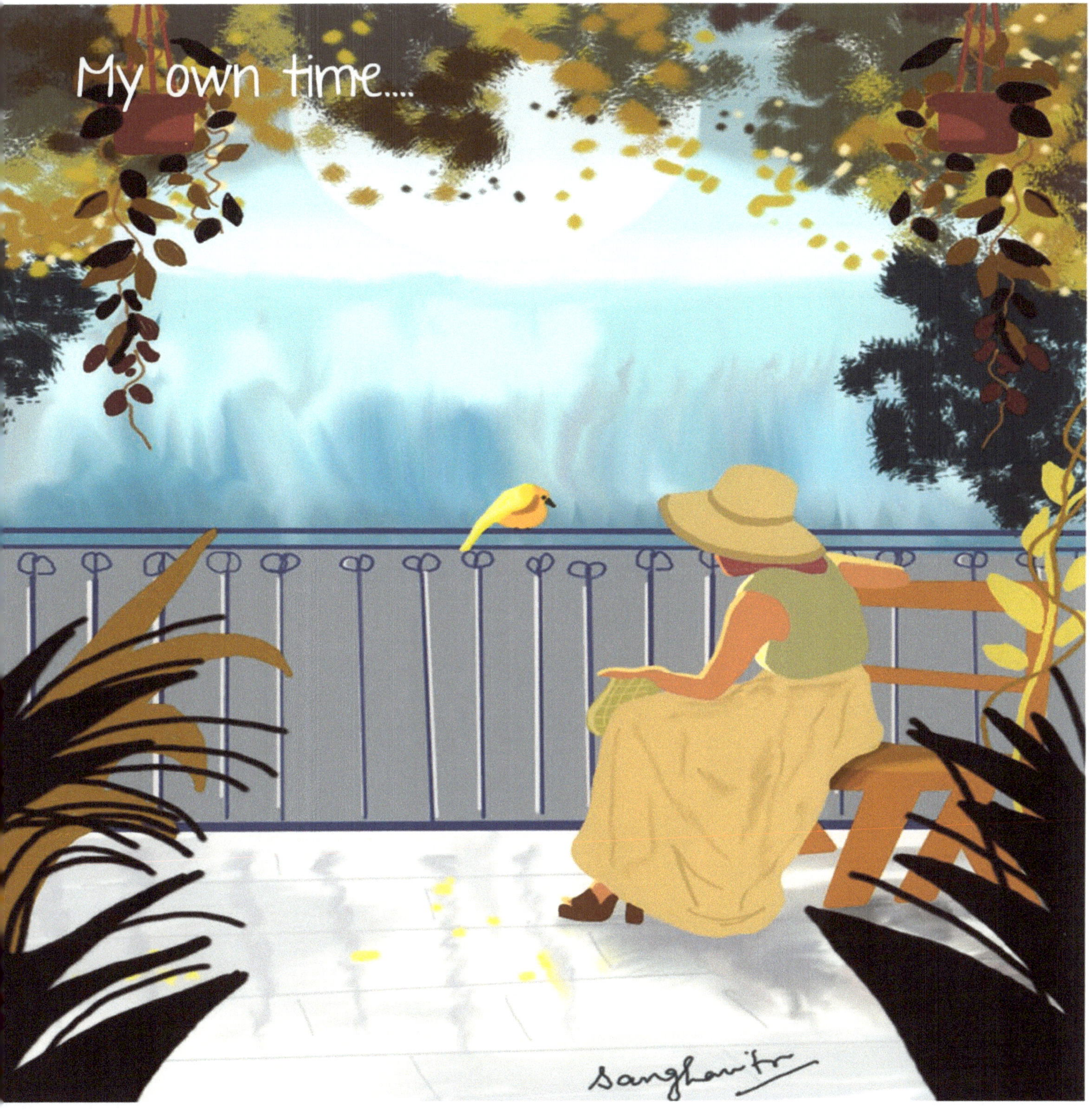
My own time....
Sanghamitra

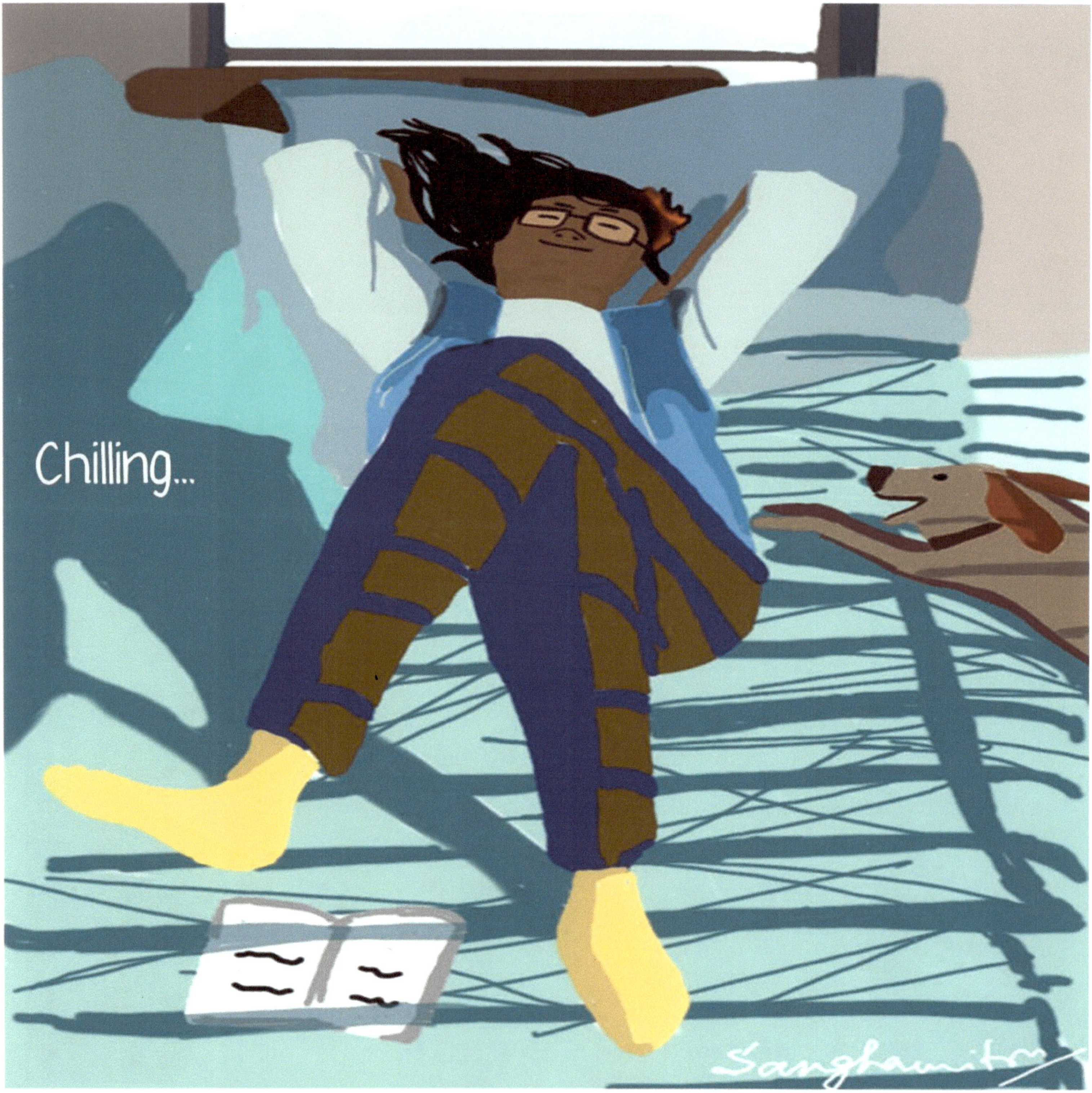
Chilling...
Sanghamitra

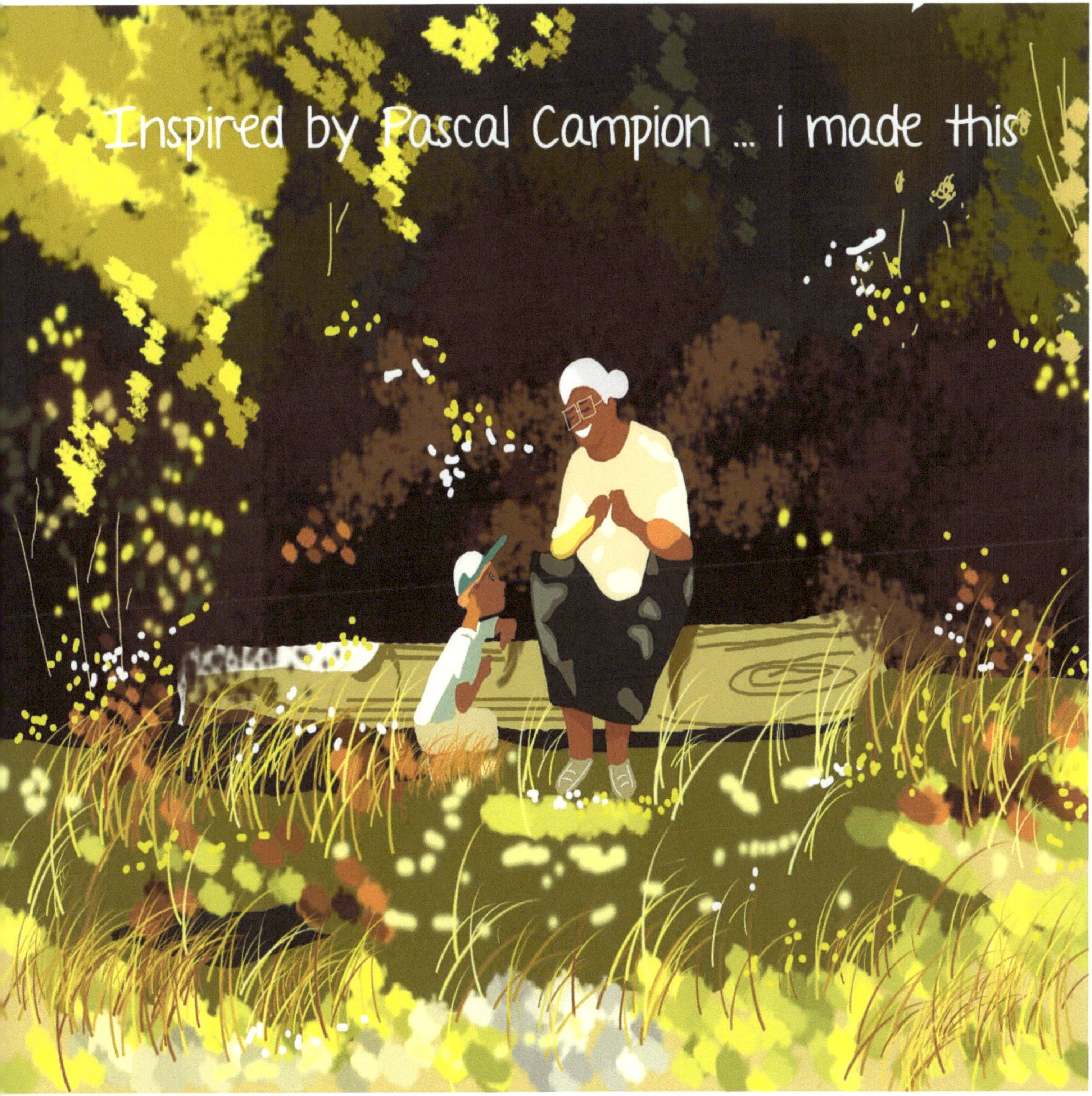
Inspired by Pascal Campion ... i made this

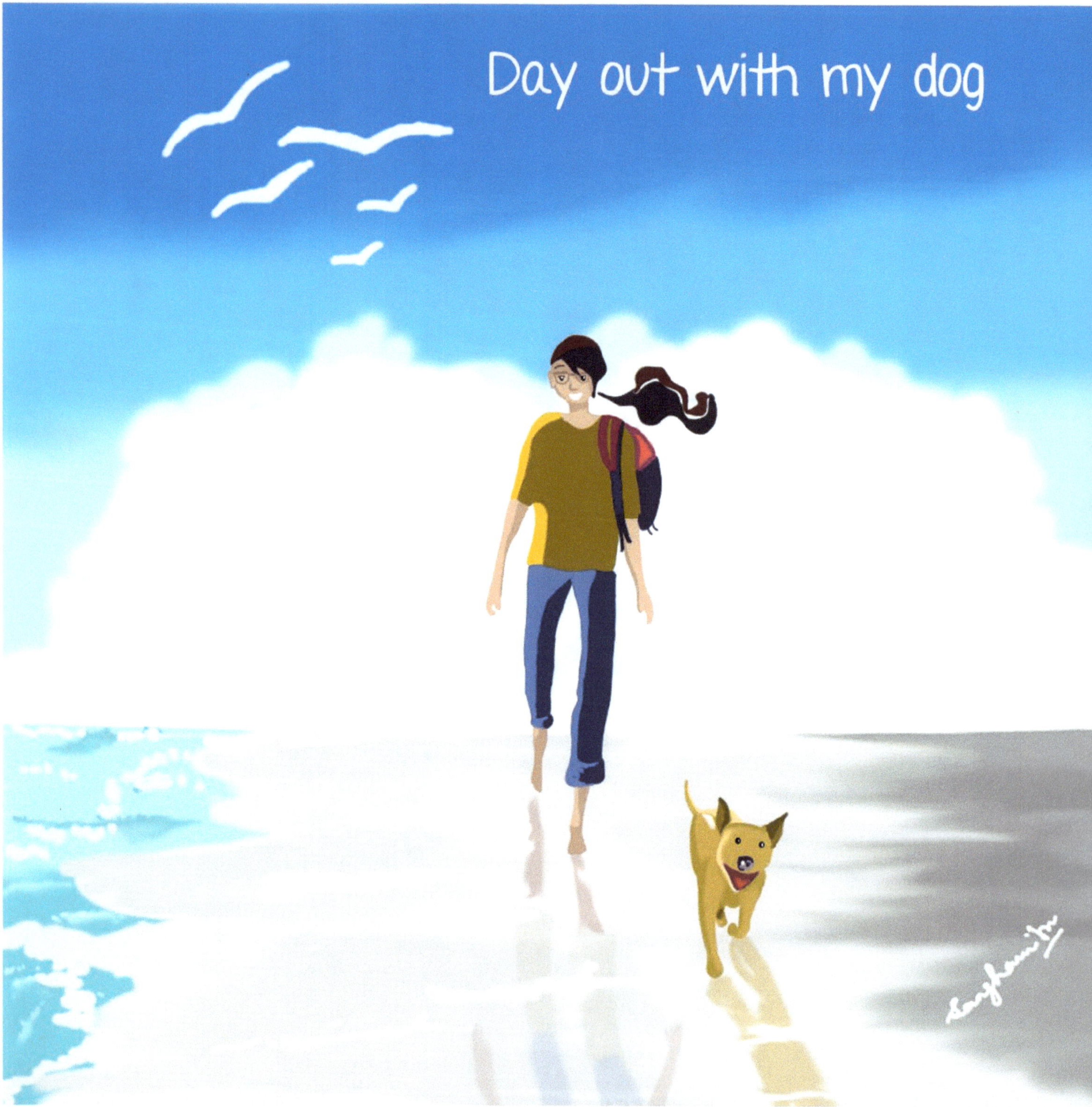
Day out with my dog

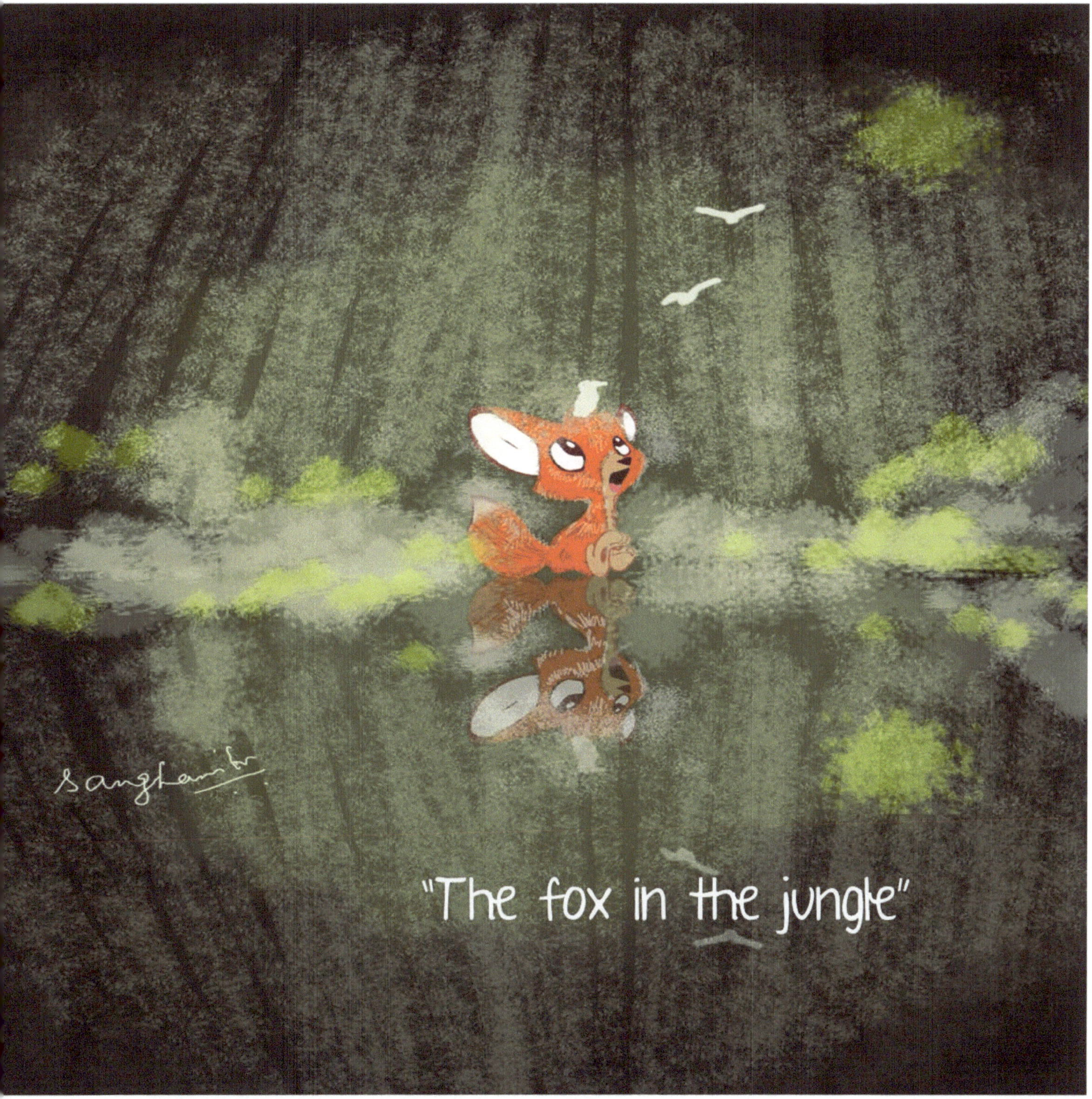
Sanghamitra
"The fox in the jungle"

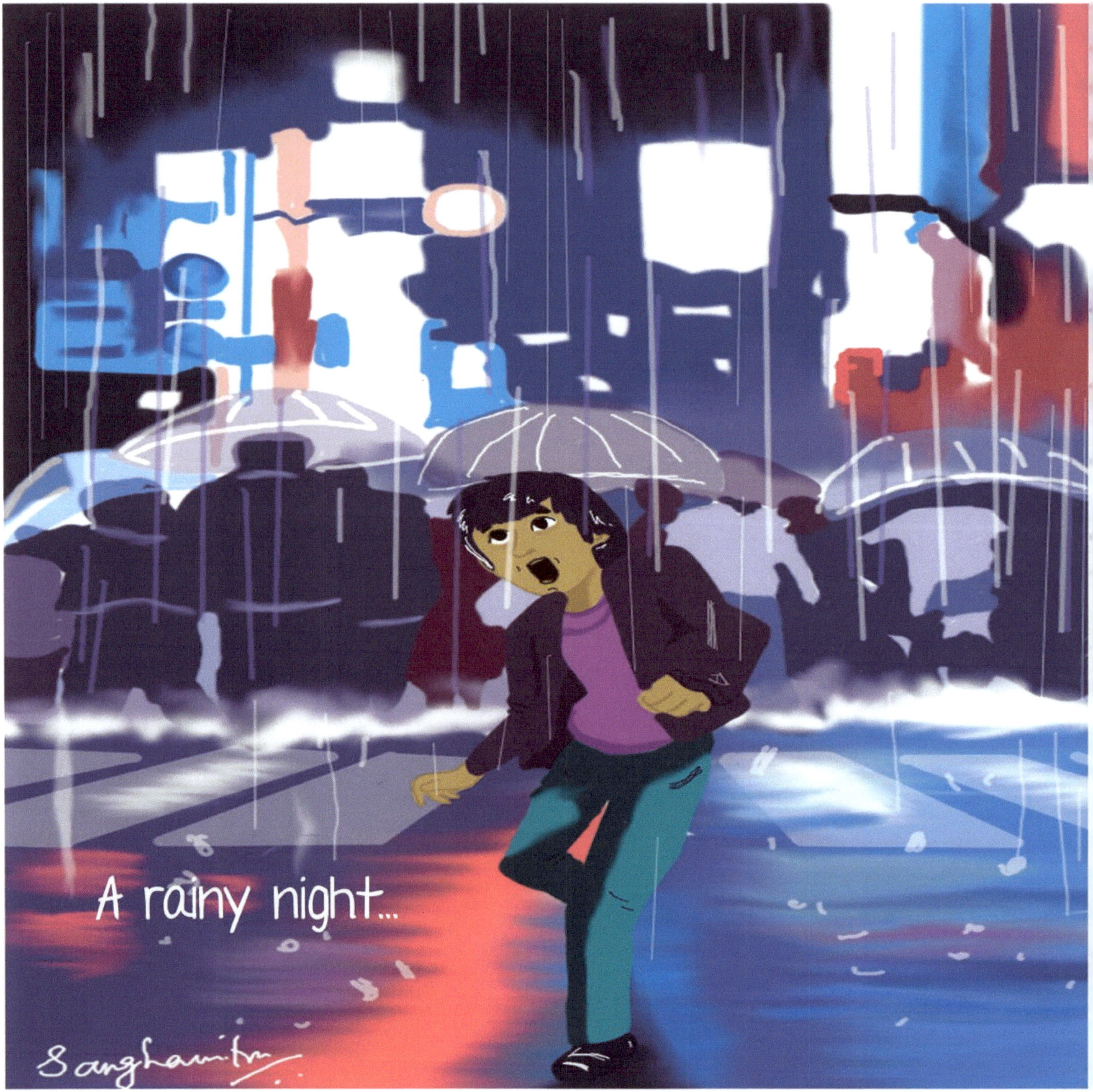
A rainy night...
Sanghamitra

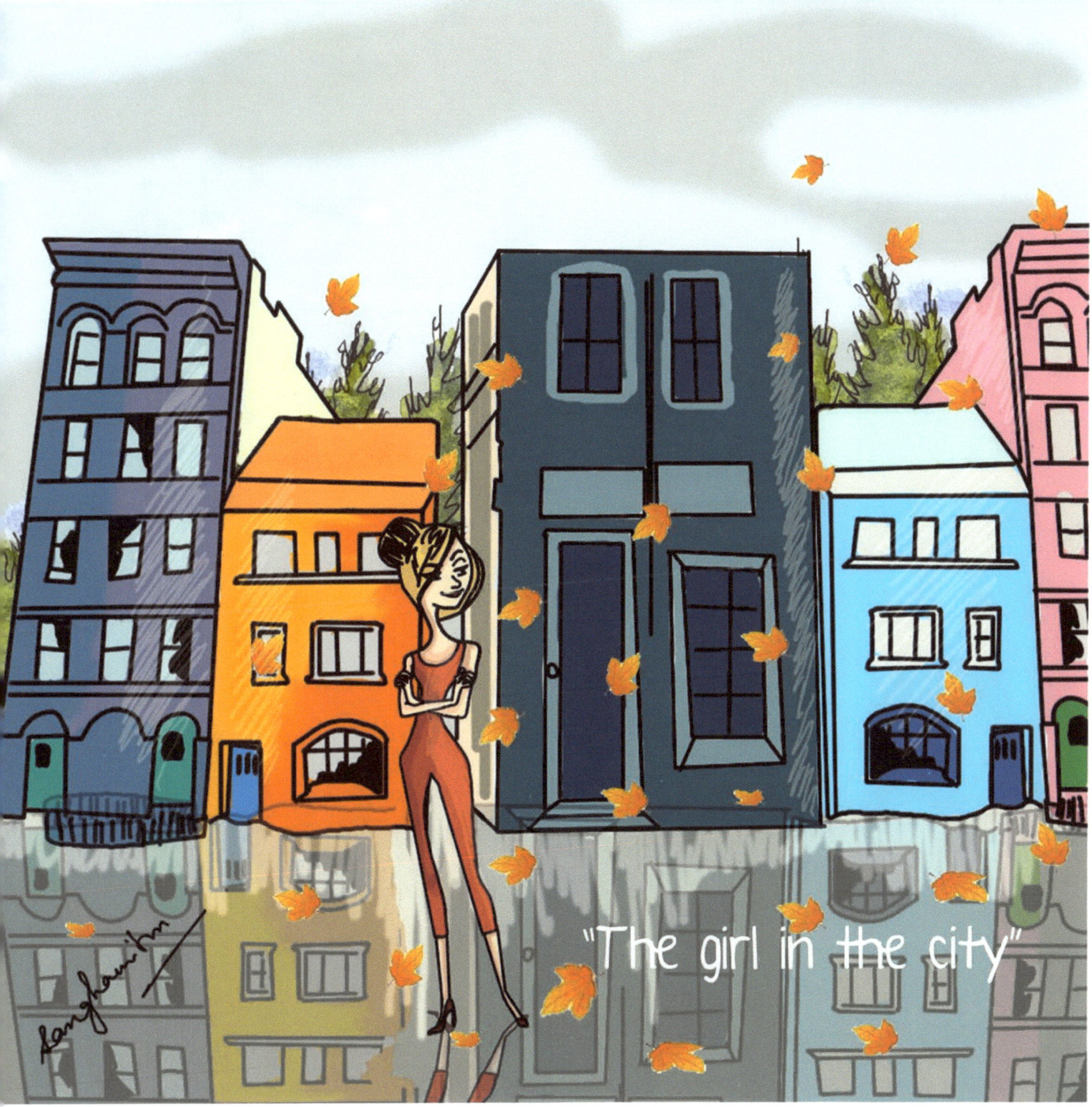
"The girl in the city"

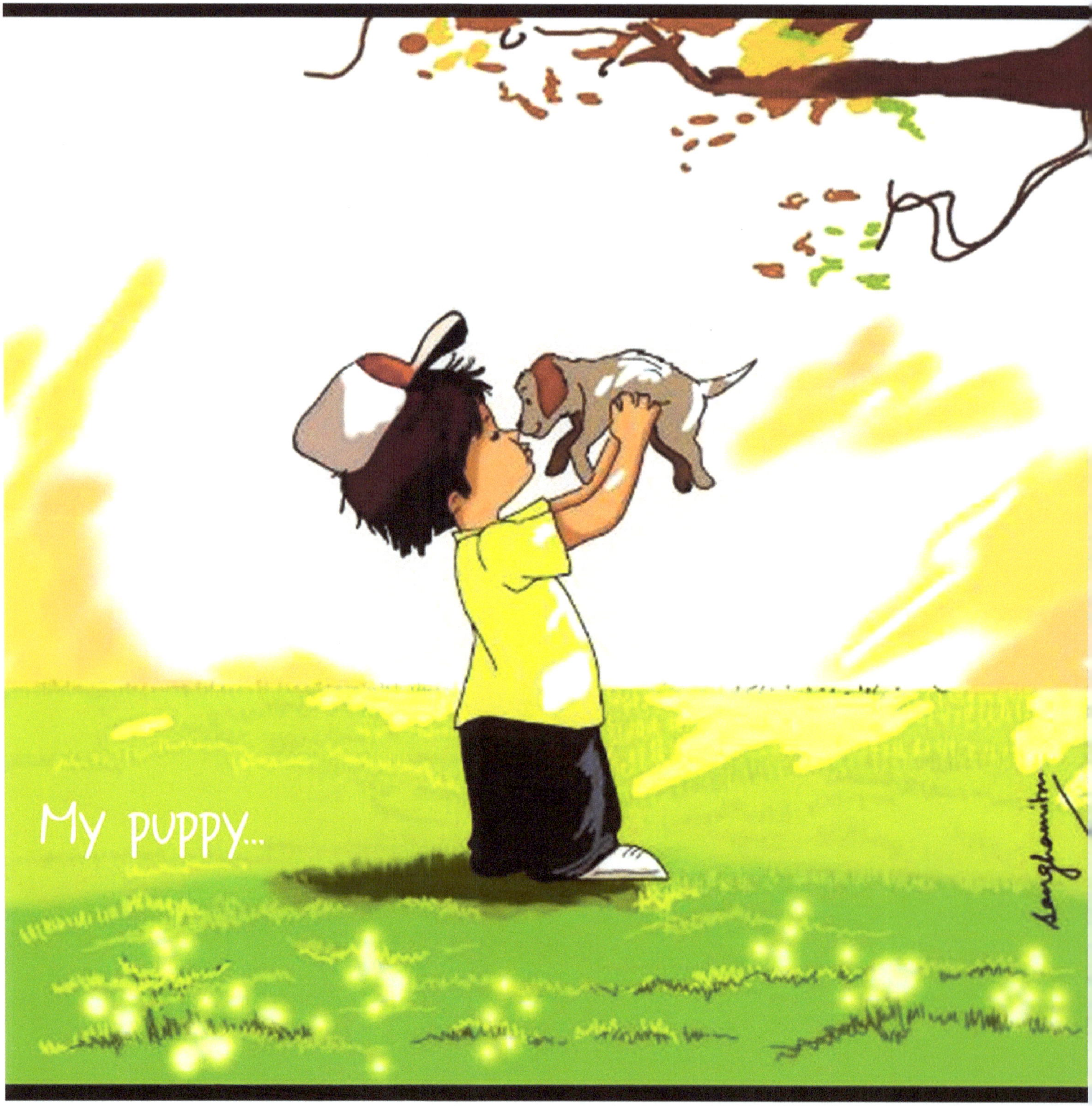
My puppy...

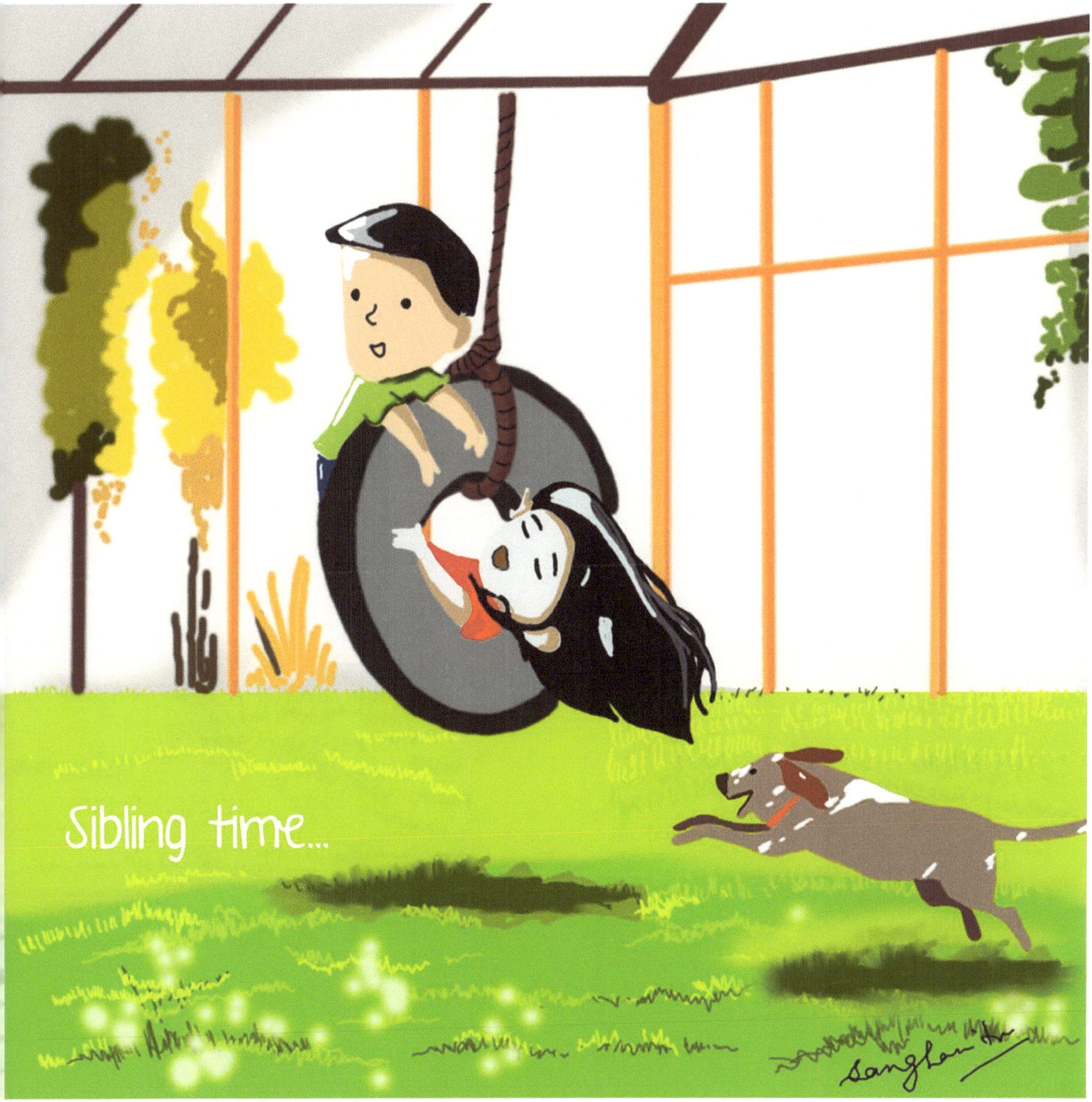
Sibling time...

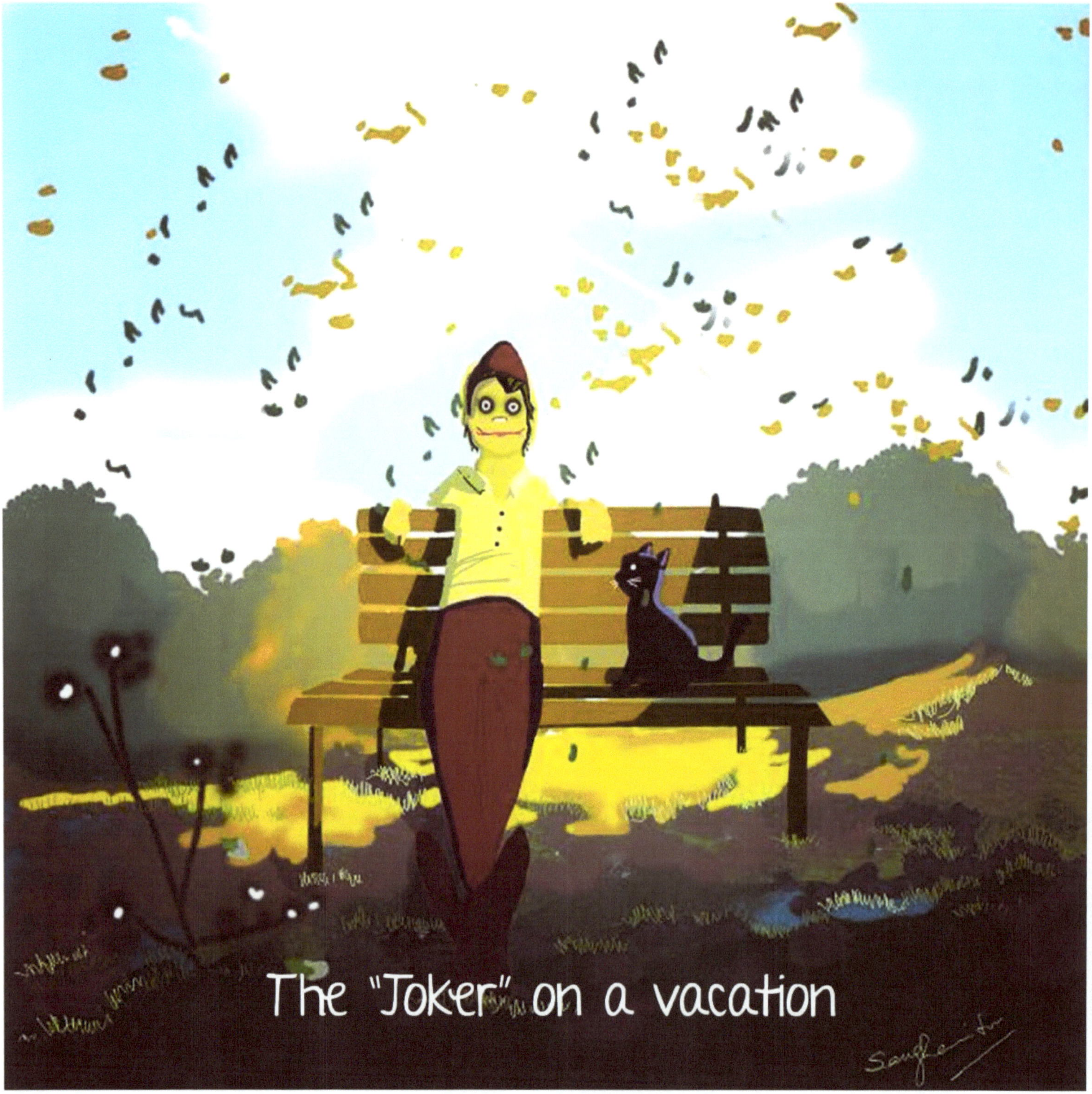
The "Joker" on a vacation

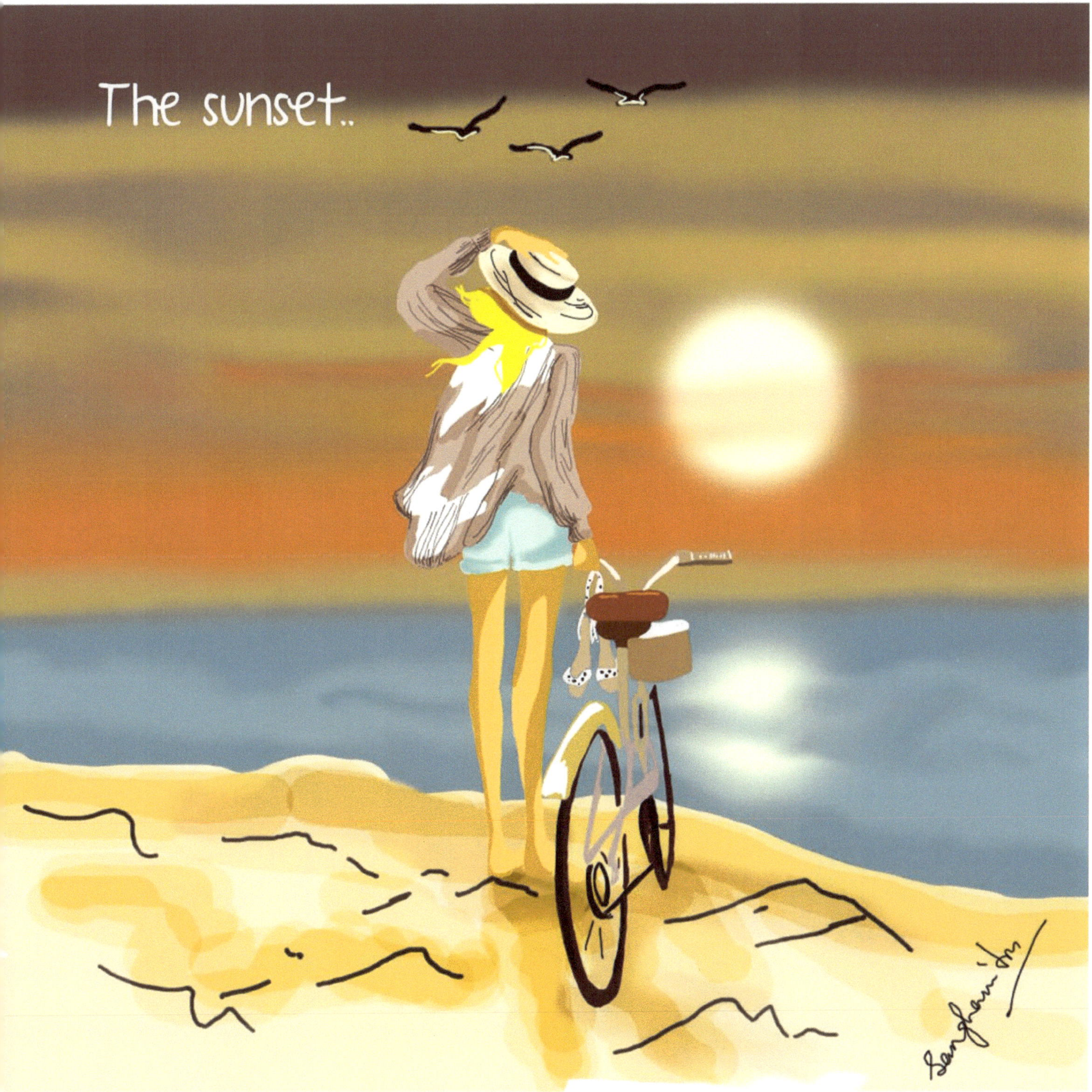
The sunset..

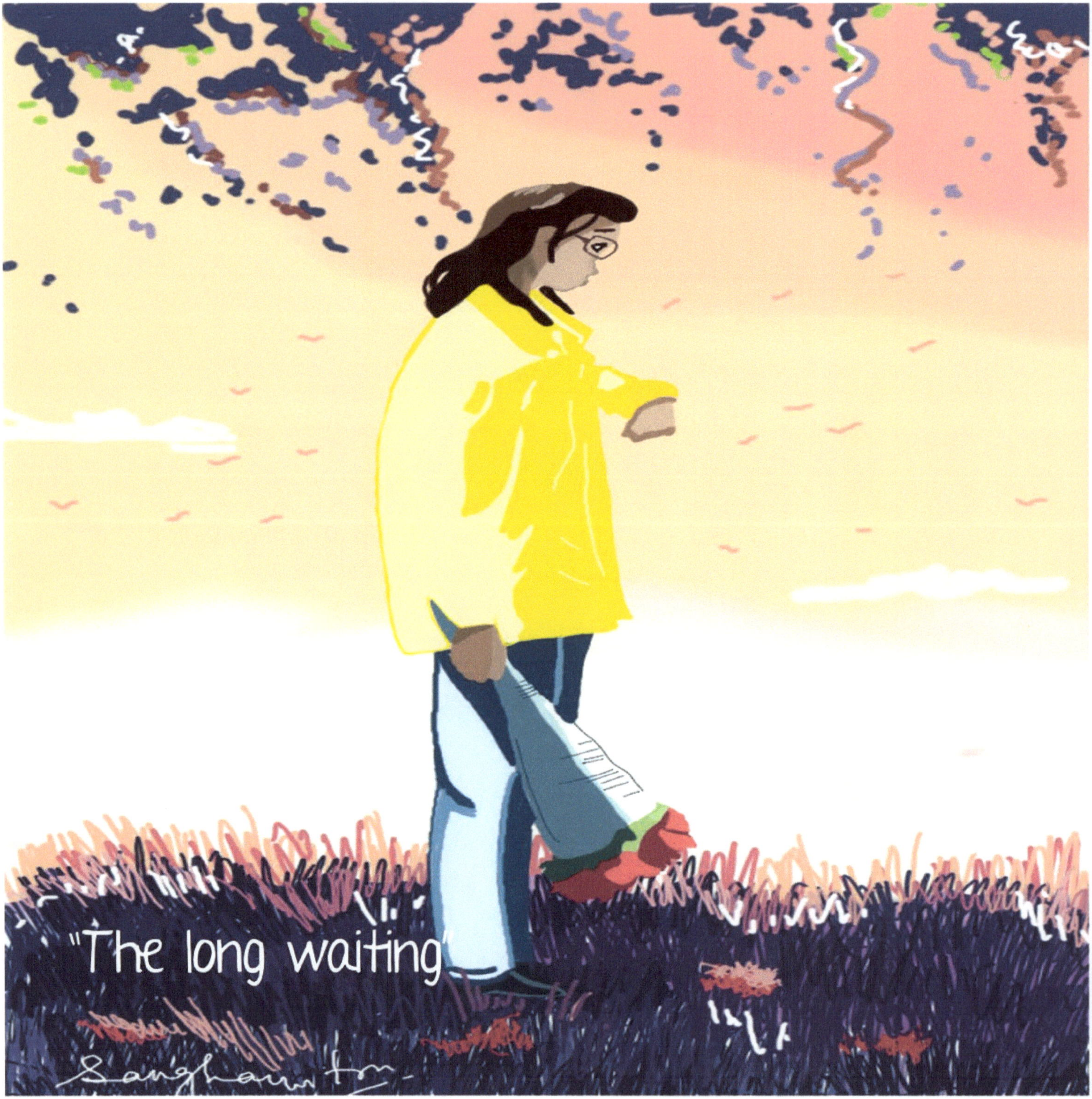
"The long waiting"

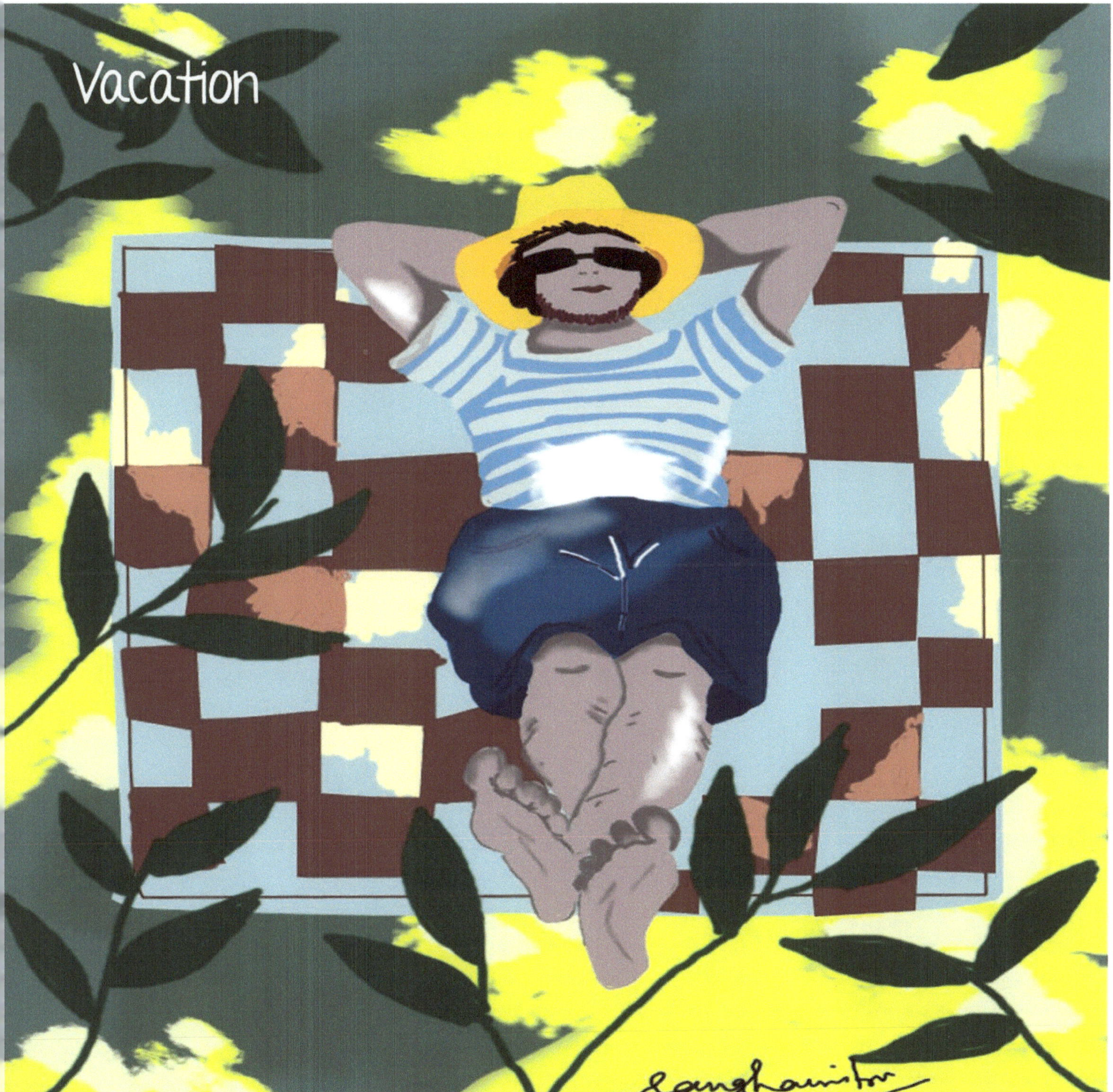
Vacation
Sanghamitra

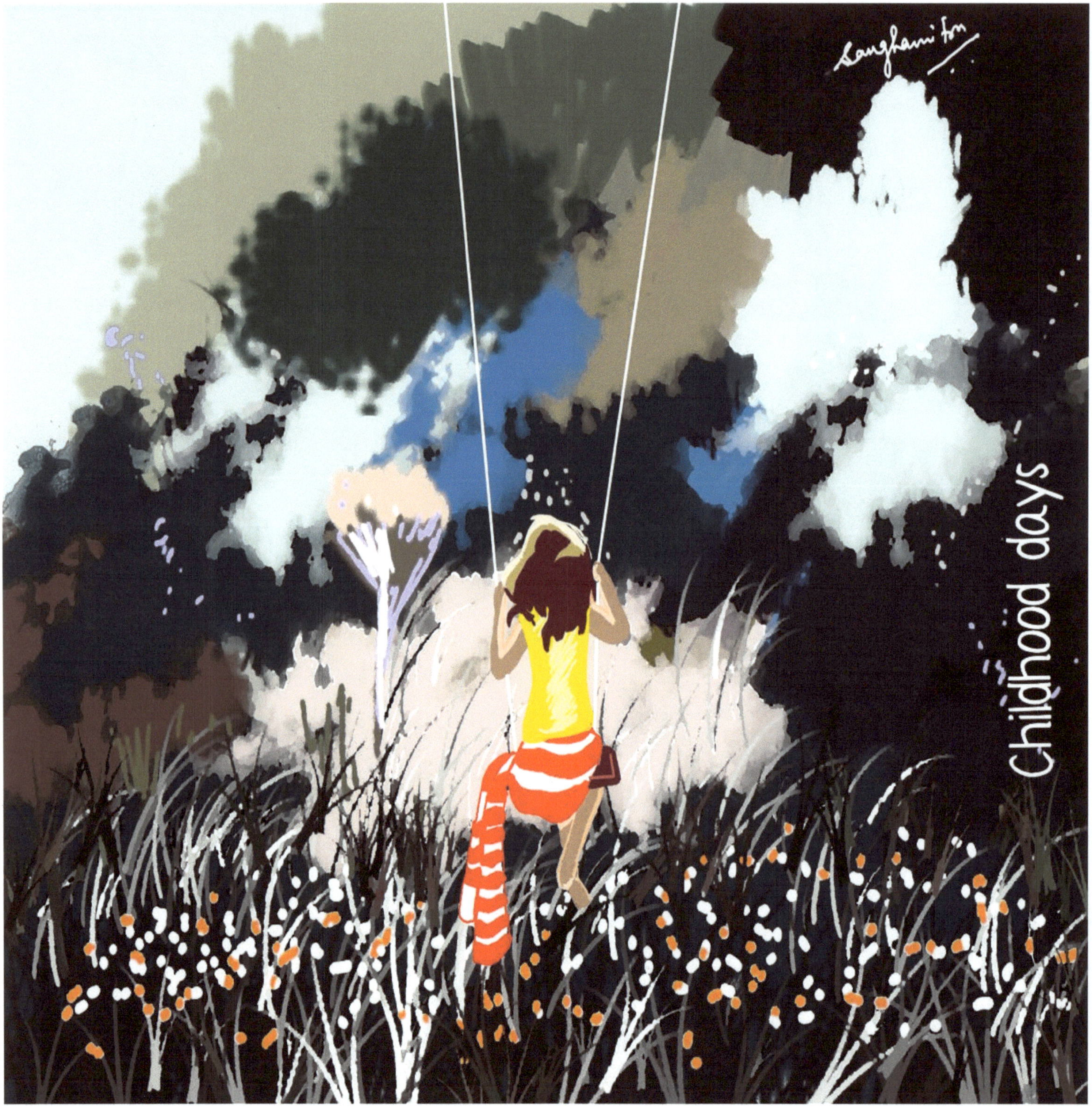
Childhood days

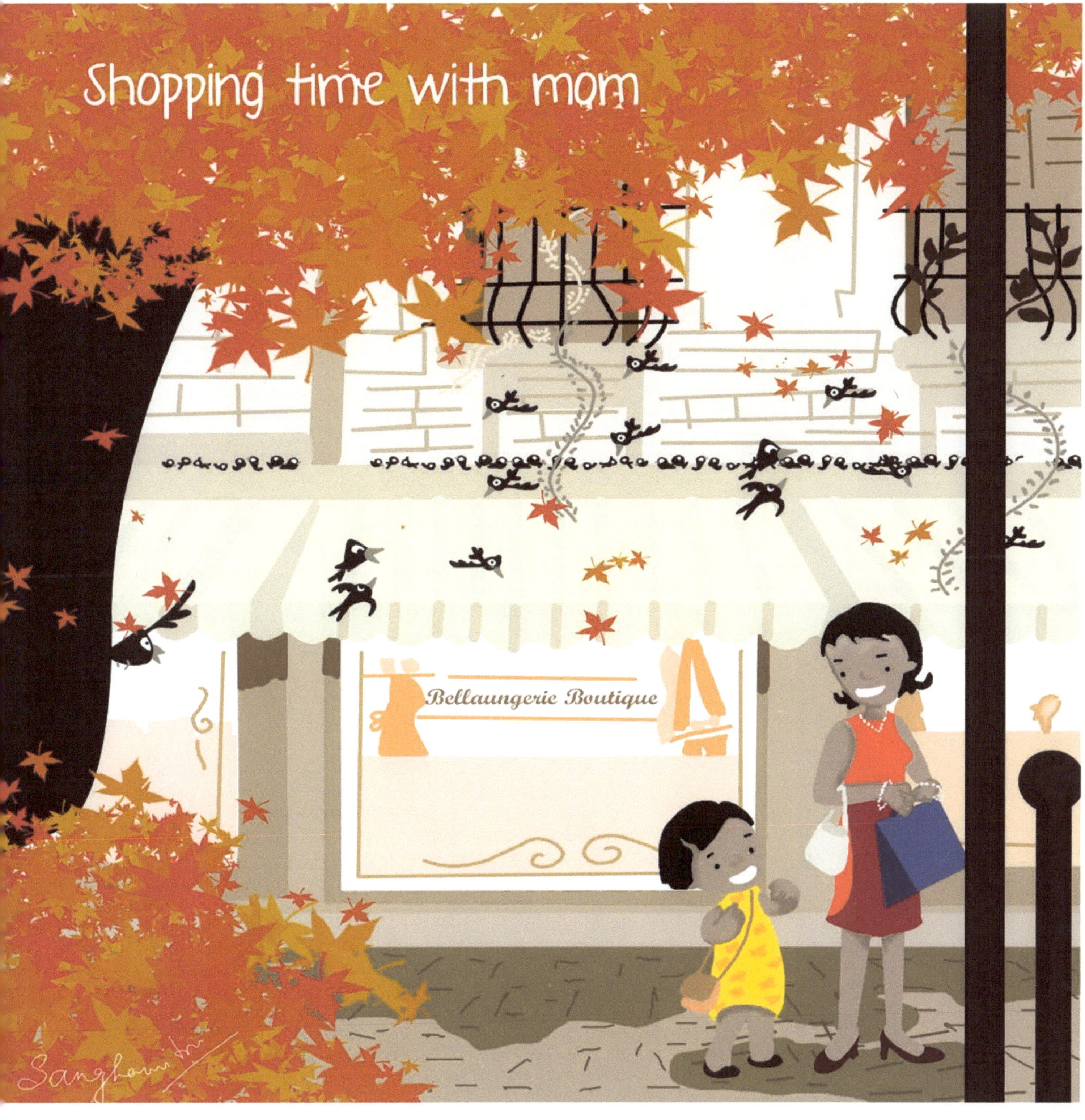
Shopping time with mom
Bellaungerie Boutique

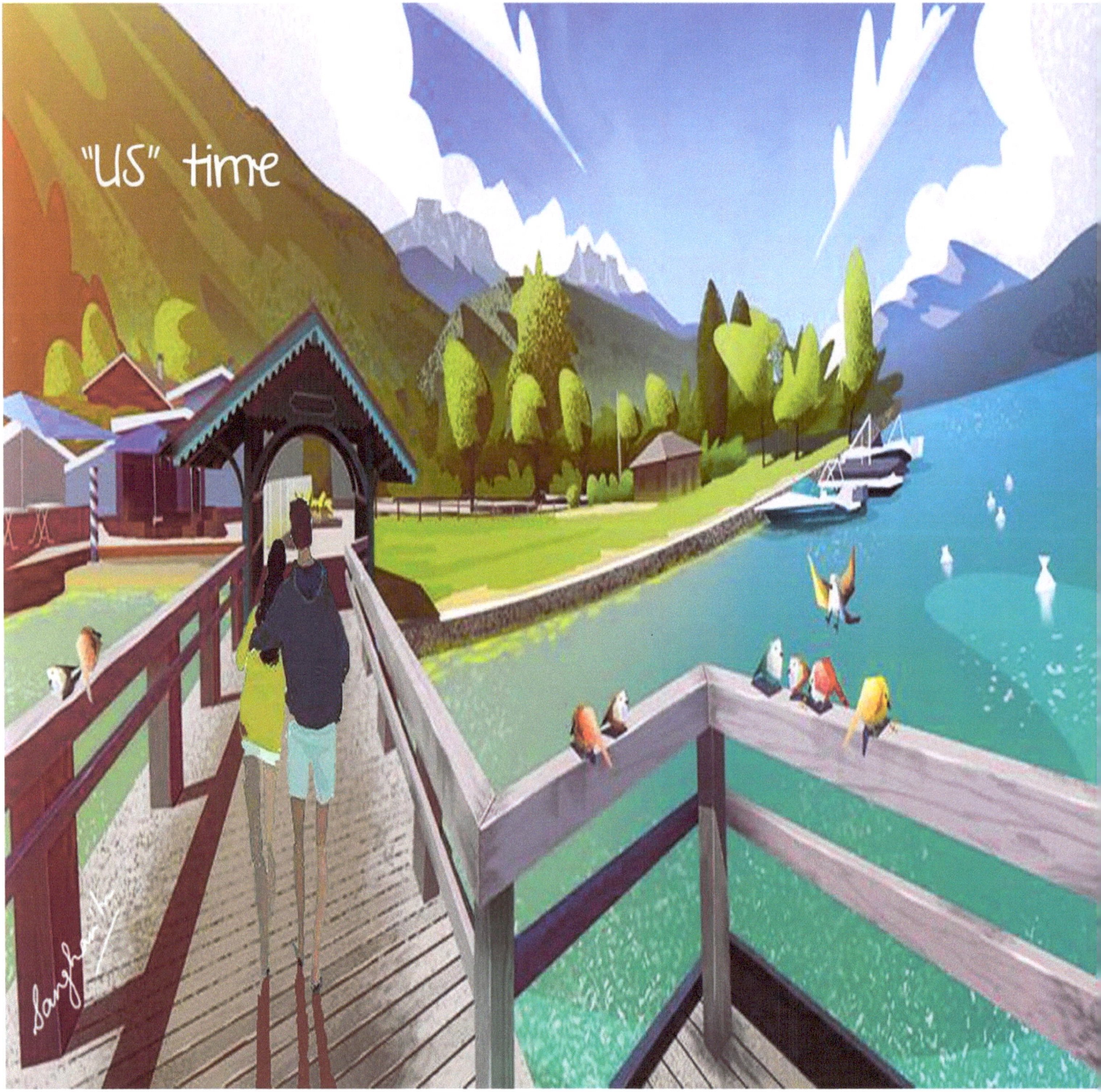
"US" time

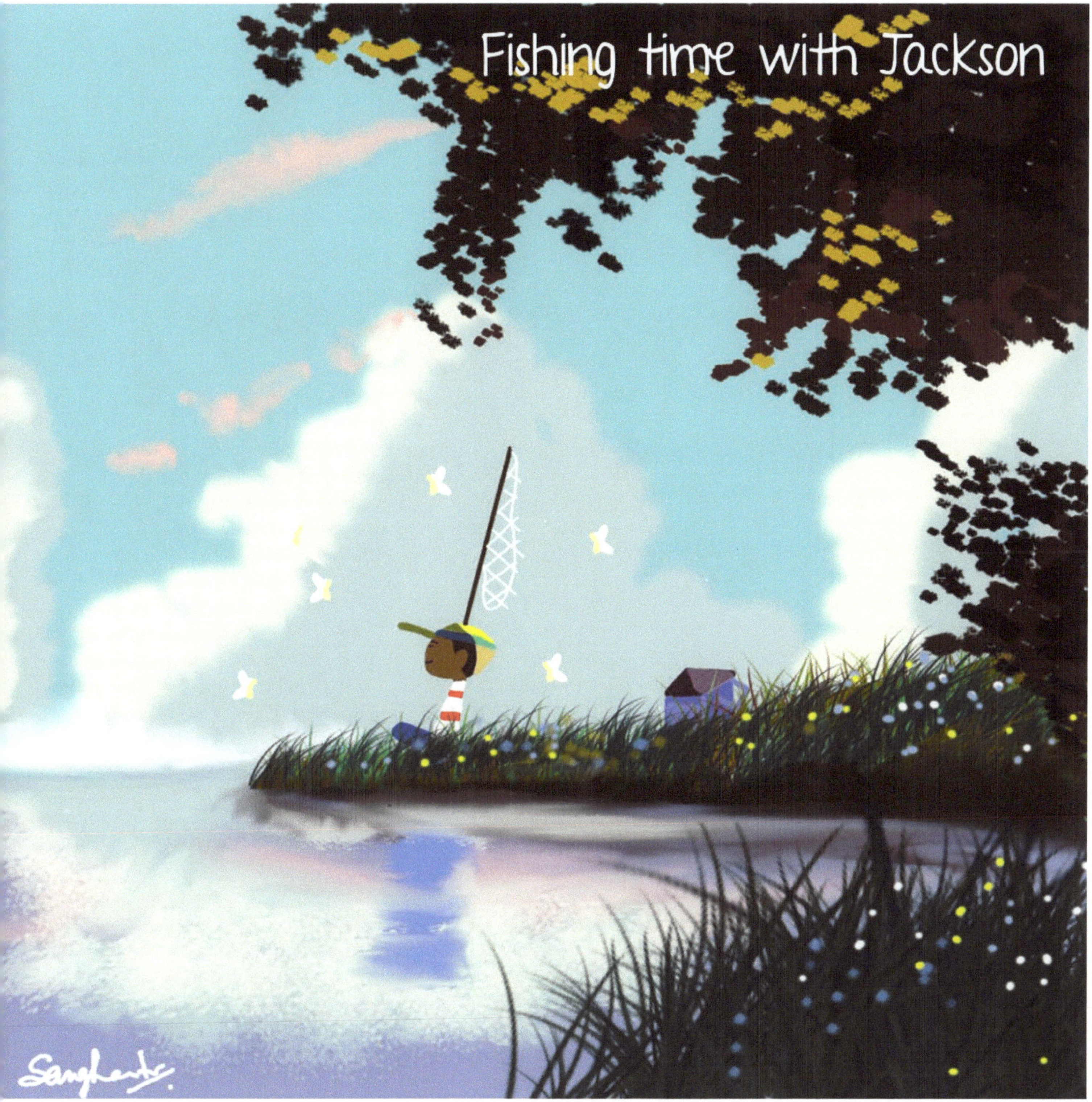
Fishing time with Jackson

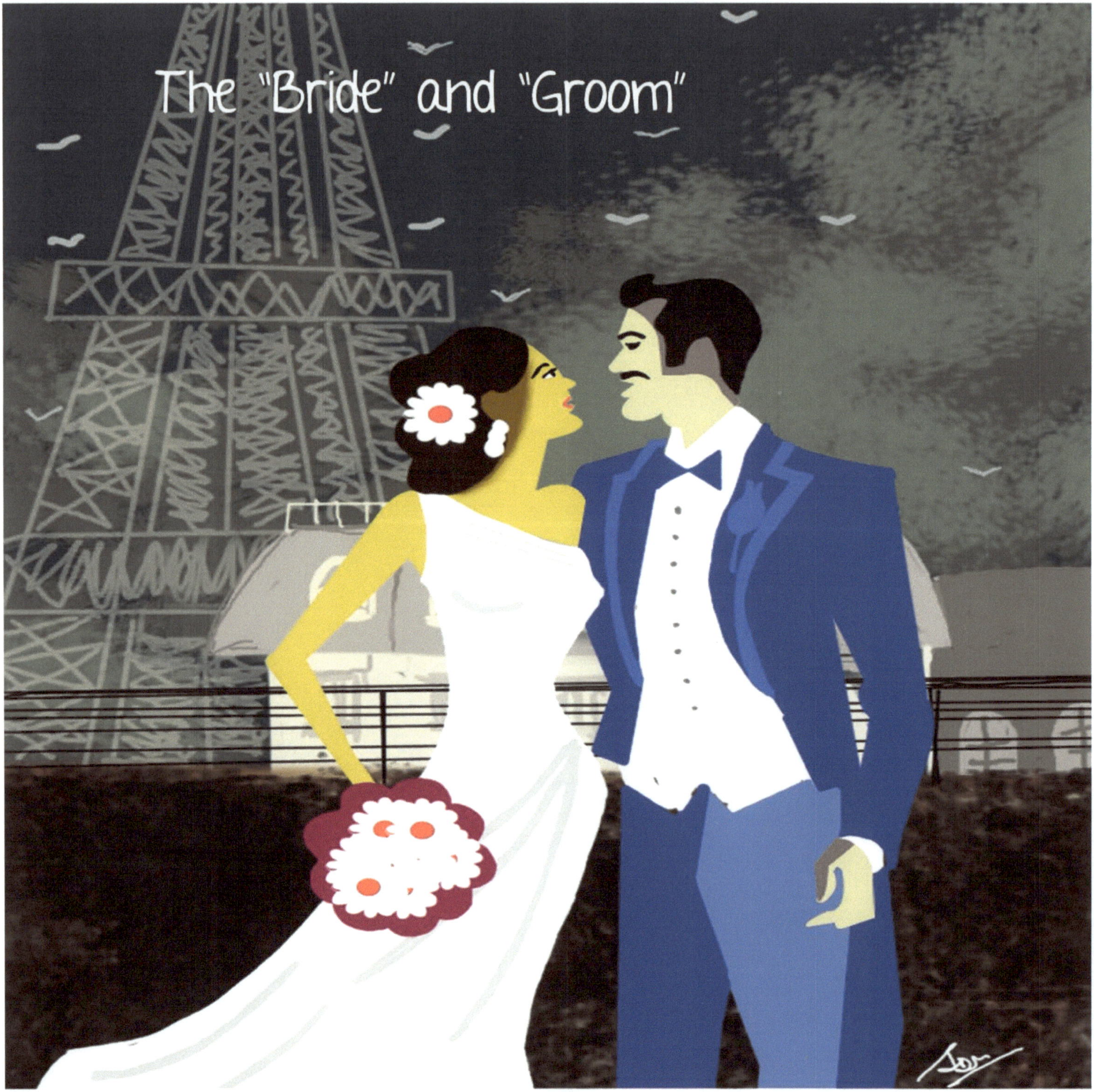
The "Bride" and "Groom"

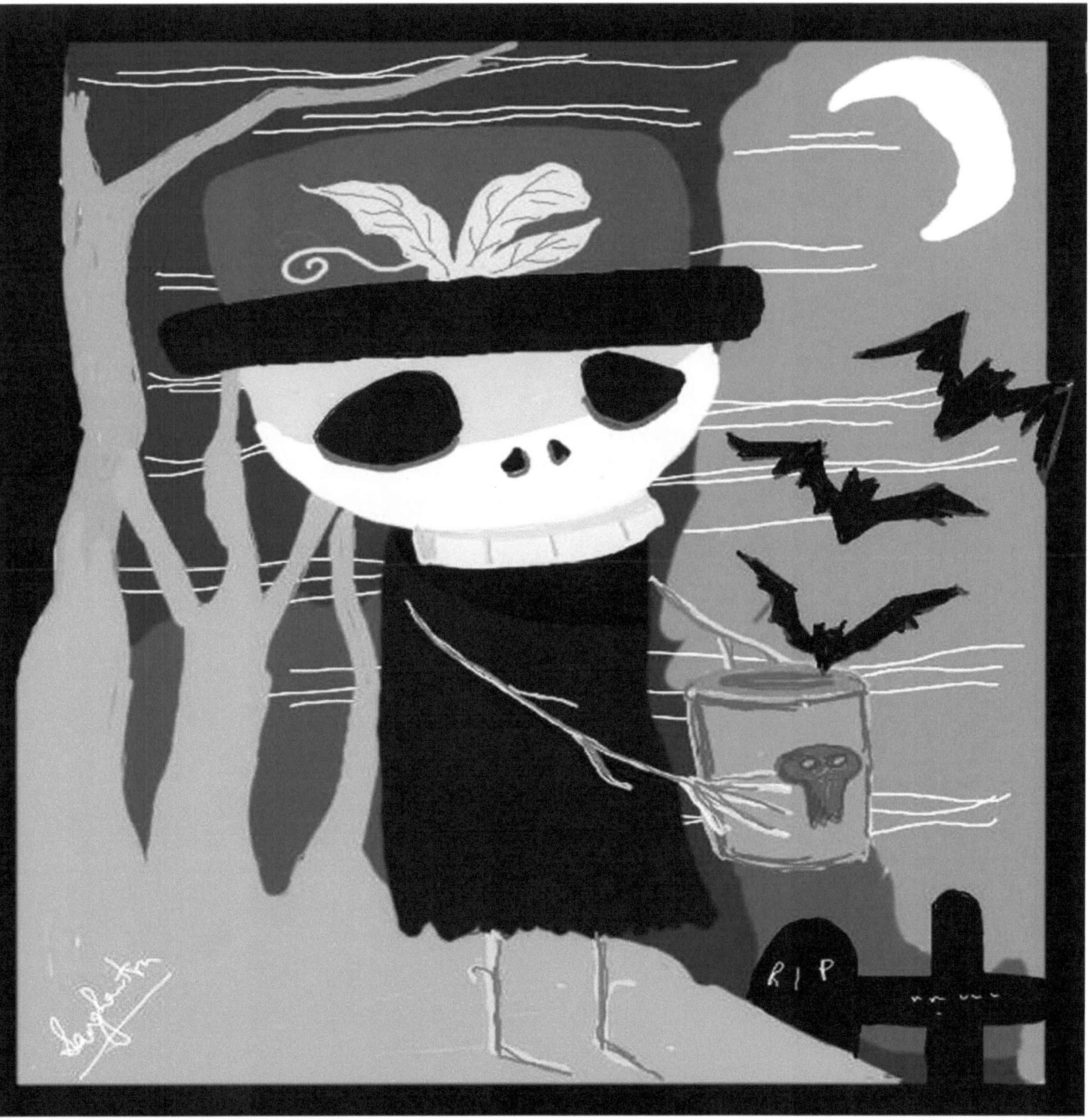
RIP

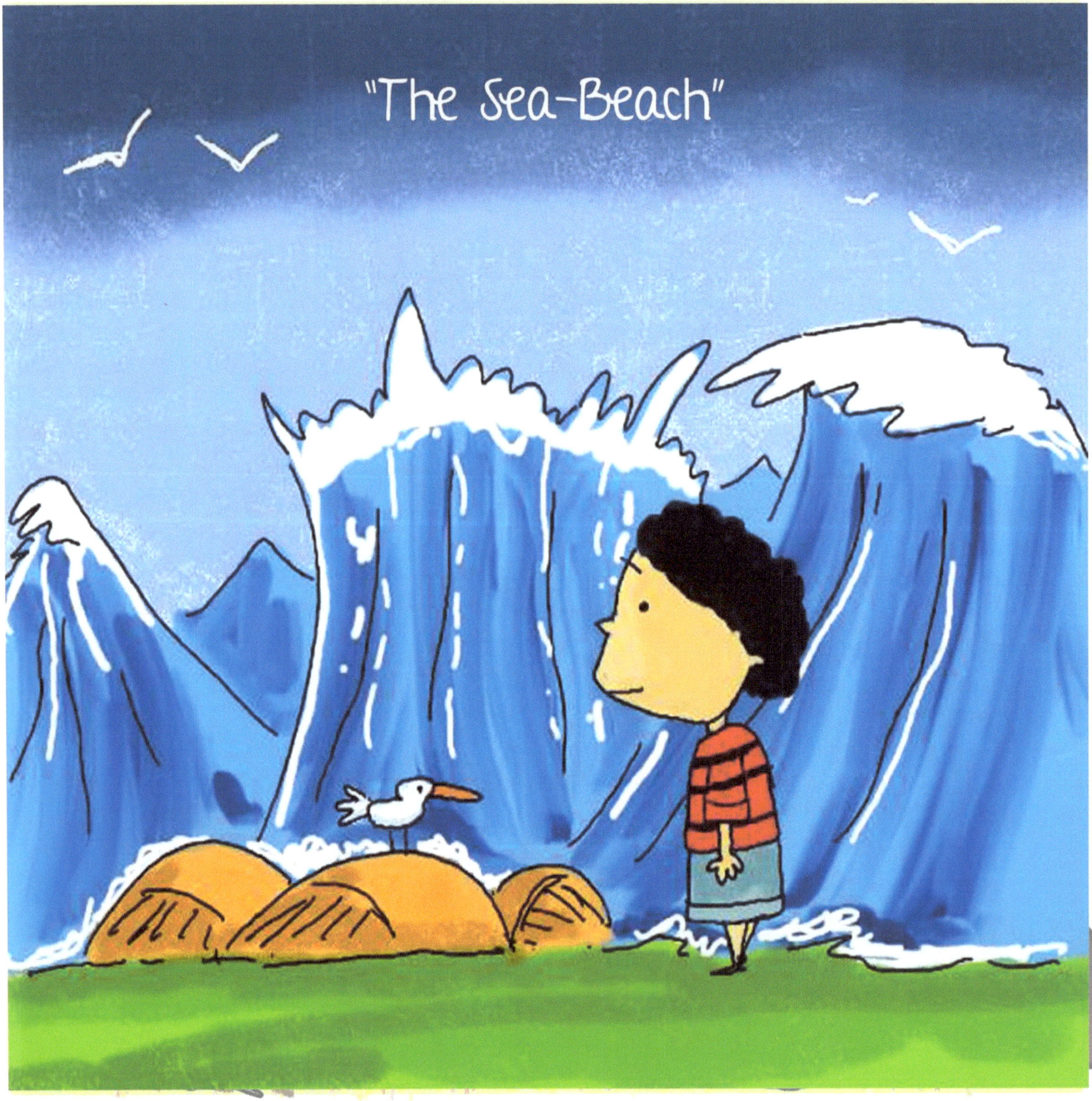
"The Sea-Beach"

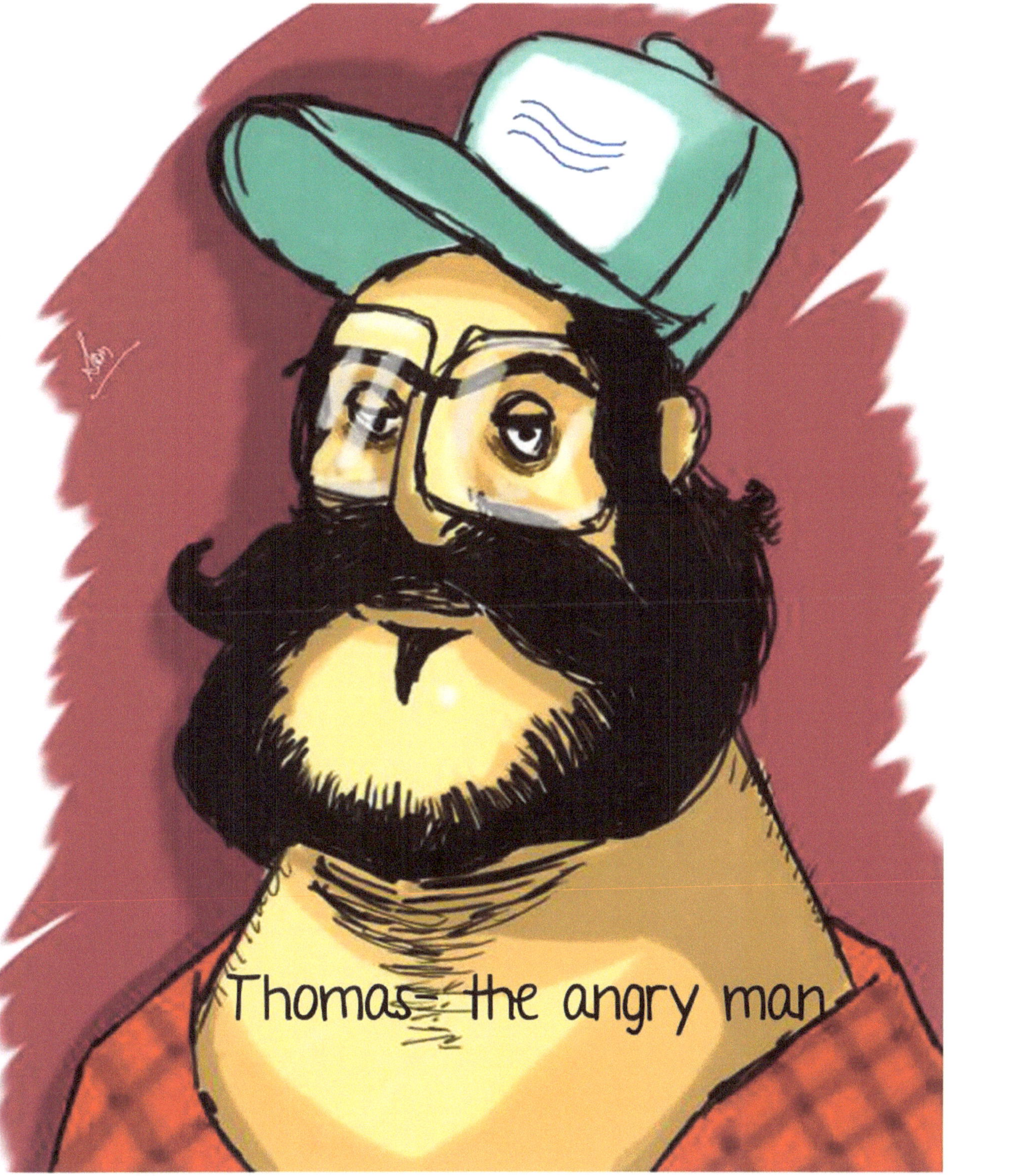
Thomas- the angry man

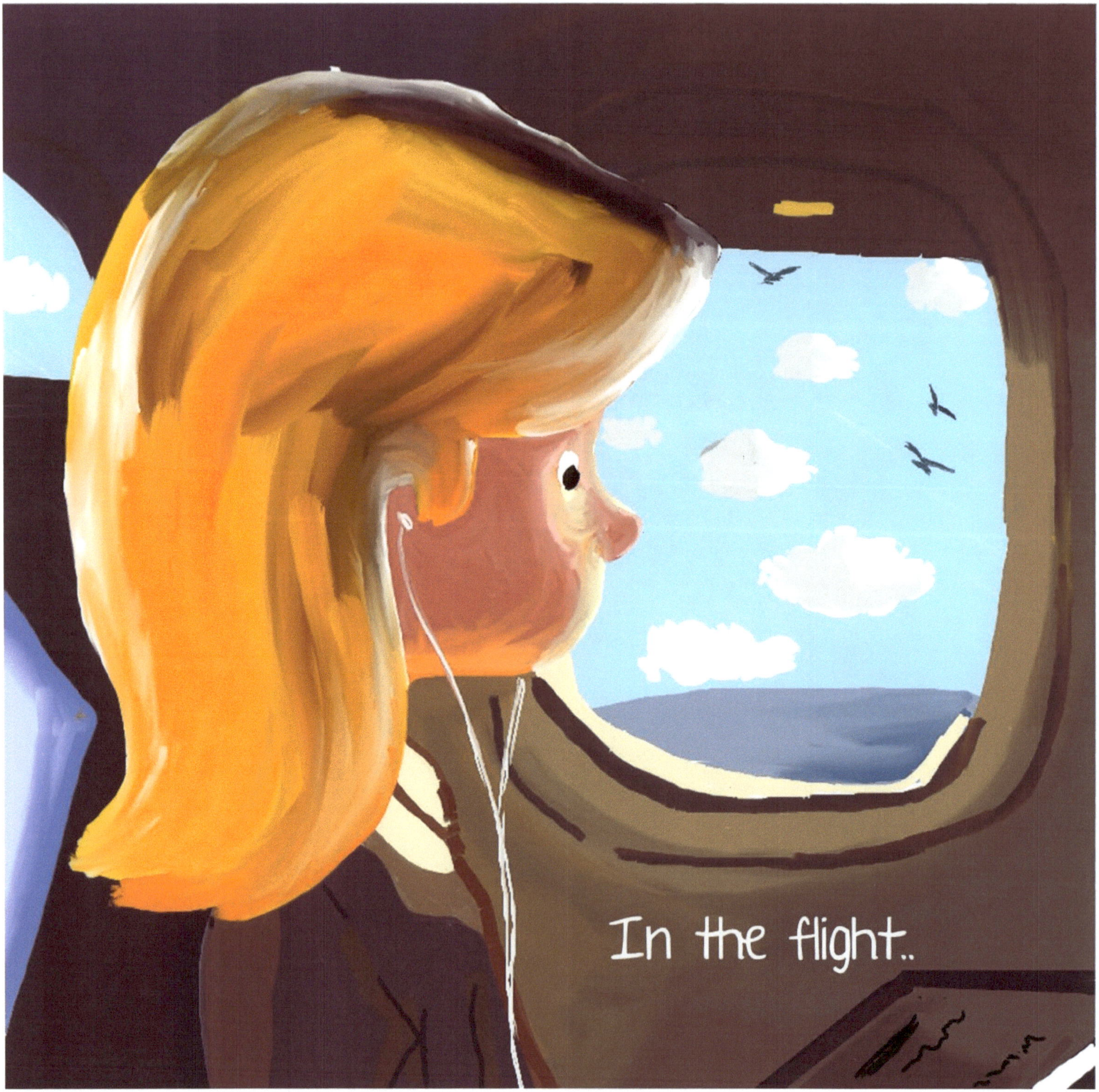
In the flight..

www.ingramcontent.com/pod-product-compliance
Lightning Source LLC
Chambersburg PA
CBHW051822210526
45473CB00005B/1700
9781986146784